Q. *In your opinion, Dr. Gustafson, what it is new?*

A. "In a sense the book is 'practical morai ~~ ology,' which seeks not to give the answer to pressing moral questions, but rather seeks to suggest ways in which answers can be responsibly found. It consistently assumes that individual 'consciences' are not to be overridden by extrinsic authority, but rather that practical moral theology requires self-examination of positions taken, reconsideration of them in the light of serious moral reflection, and that persuasiveness is the means of power to be exercised in persons coming to a point of view, or in changing a point of view."

For those interested in the work of one of America's most destinyminded and recognized scholars in the field of theological ethics, this volume is a rare treat indeed. The introduction by Charles M. Swezey, provides a cogent introduction not merely to this book, but to the Gustafson corpus in general. By showing how THE CHURCH AS MORAL DECISION-MAKER is the practical application to the core of Gustafson's thought to date, and how his ideas about the church as community are applied to the social phenomena in this morning's headlines, Mr. Swezey provides a signal service both to beginning and devoted readers of Gustafson.

JAMES M. GUSTAFSON is Professor of Ethics at Yale University, teaching in both the Divinity School and the Graduate School of Religion. He is a graduate of the University of Chicago (B.A., B.D.) and Yale (Ph.D.) and a minister in the United Church of Christ. He is the author of TREASURE IN EARTHEN VESSELS: The Church as a Human Community, CHRIST AND THE MORAL LIFE, co-author with H. Richard Niebuhr and D. D. Williams, THE ADVANCEMENT OF THEOLOGICAL EDUCATION, and co-editor of ON BEING RESPONSIBLE.

THE CHURCH
AS MORAL
DECISION-MAKER

THE CHURCH AS MORAL DECISION-MAKER

James M. Gustafson

Pilgrim Press/Philadelphia/Boston

SBN 8298-0178-2

Library of Congress Catalog Card Number 74-124454

The author gratefully acknowledges and expresses appreciation to the following publishers and journals for permission to reprint material originally published as follows:

"Christian Attitudes Toward a Technological Society" in *Theology Today*, July 1959, Vol. XVI, No. 2.

"Patterns of Christian Social Action" in *Theology Today*, July 1961, Vol. XVIII, No. 2.

"Authority in Pluralistic Society" in *Lutheran World*, Jan. 1963, Vol. X, No. 1, published by the Lutheran World Federation.

"A Theology of Christian Community" in *Man in Community: Christian Concern for the Human in Changing Society*, ed. Egbert de Vries (New York: Association Press, 1966).

"The Church: A Community of Moral Discourse" in *The Crane Review*, Winter 1964, Vol. VI, No. 2.

"Churchmen as God's Deputies" (excerpts from "Christian Conviction and Christian Action") in *The Presbyterian Outlook*, Sept. 14, 1964, Vol. 146, No. 32. The entire essay was printed in *Presbyterian Action*, Jan. and Feb. 1965, Vol. 15, Nos. 1 and 2.

"The Voluntary Church: A Moral Appraisal" in *Voluntary Associations: A Study of Groups in Free Societies*, ed. D. B. Robertson (Richmond: John Knox Press, 1966). © M. E. Bratcher 1966.

"Foundations of Ministry," reprinted from *The Church and Its Manpower Management:* (1966) A Report of the First National Consultation on Church Personnel Policies and Practices, edited by Ross P. Scherer and Theodore O. Wedel. Published for the Department of Ministry, Vocation, and Pastoral Services, Division of Christian Education by the Department of Publication Services of the National Council of the Churches of Christ in the U.S.A. Used with permission.

"Two Requisites for the American Church: Moral Discourse and Institutional Power" in *The Future of the American Church*, ed. Philip J. Hefner (Philadelphia: Fortress Press, 1968).

For three great teachers of Christian ethics
TWO IN REVERED MEMORY:
H. Richard Niebuhr 1894–1962
Kenneth W. Underwood 1918–1968
ONE IN ACTIVE RETIREMENT:
James Luther Adams

Contents

THE CHURCH
AS MORAL
DECISION-MAKER

Introduction

Part One

James M. Gustafson has written a wide variety of articles pertaining to theological ethics which have appeared in a number of books, periodicals, and professional journals since he joined the faculty at Yale University in 1955. The nine essays collected here concern the church as a moral community. While this introduction is not the place either for an extended critique or for a laudatory exposition of the Gustafson corpus, I can nonetheless take this opportunity to indicate a perspective from which these articles may be viewed which is not out of accord with the rest of what Gustafson has written.

Most contemporary theological ethicists are acutely aware, even highly self conscious of the fact, that one's definition or understanding of the discipline of ethics determines in large measure what data are considered relevant for ethical inquiry. It is a truism that the categories selected with which to "do ethics" fashion and limit the levels of discourse and the types of material deemed appropriate to the discipline. Indeed, one may observe that the conceptual problem of defining the proper frames of reference for theological ethics (and the way one then executes his task within the given frames of reference) is one of the most pressing issues within the discipline at the present time. Certainly there is no available or emerging consensus. Gustafson has suggested a variety of ways in which one can proceed to do ethics.

In an early article in the H. Richard Niebuhr *Festschrift*,[1] for example, Gustafson suggested that there are three starting points for Christian social ethics (Christian revelation and faith, an analysis of the self, and an understanding of social structures and processes), and he therefore asserts that in theological-ethical discourse there is "more than one premise to the argument." In his well-known essay, "Context Versus Principles: A Misplaced Debate in Christian Ethics," [2] Gustafson suggested that the discipline of Christian ethics "can and does" proceed from at least four bases or starting points (social analysis, theological affirmations, moral principles, and the nature of the Christian's life in Christ). Gustafson has also made a number of other suggestions concerning how one can conceive of the discipline of theological ethics.

In his major book to date, *Christ and the Moral Life*,[3] Gustafson proposes three categories as being "almost" intrinsic to all ethical inquiry.[4] The scheme is developed by first asking the existential question all conscientious moral persons ask, i.e., What ought I to do? The suggestion is that if one begins ethical analysis with this personal question, he will find that it leads him— on other levels of discourse—to three substantive concerns. These three concerns, in turn, can be correlated to the claims that theologians make or apparently assume for the significance of Christ for the moral life. Thus, if one pursues the question, What ought I to do? he finds that he is asking a question concerning the nature of the good or the locus of value. Hence Gustafson devotes a chapter of his book to a critical exposition of how various theo-

---

[1] James M. Gustafson, "Christian Ethics and Social Policy," *Faith and Ethics: The Theology of H. Richard Niebuhr*, ed. Paul Ramsey (New York: Harper & Bros., 1957), pp. 119–39.

[2] James M. Gustafson, "Context Versus Principles: A Misplaced Debate in Christian Ethics," *New Theology*, No. 3, ed. Martin E. Marty and Dean G. Peerman (New York: Macmillan, 1966), pp. 69–102.

[3] James M. Gustafson, *Christ and the Moral Life* (New York: Harper & Row, 1968), 275 pp.

[4] The three categories are set forth briefly but more explicitly in James M. Gustafson, "Theology and Ethics," *The Scope of Theology*, ed. Daniel T. Jenkins (Cleveland: World Publishing Co., 1965), pp. 111–32.

logians have viewed Jesus Christ (as the Lord who is Creator and Redeemer) as a source of moral goodness that can be relied upon. Again, if one pursues the question, What ought I to do? he discovers that he is asking a question about the nature and character of the moral agent. Hence Gustafson devotes two chapters of his book to a critical exposition of how theologians have viewed Jesus Christ (as Justifier and Sanctifier) in respect to the way in which Christ conditions or determines what the moral agent has become and is as a person. Finally, if one pursues the question, What ought I to do? he becomes aware that he is asking a question concerning the principles, or the models used for moral guidance. Hence Gustafson devotes two chapters of his book to a critical exposition of how various theologians have viewed Jesus Christ (as Pattern and Teacher) in respect to the example Christ provides for the moral lives of Christians and in respect to the ways Christ's teachings have been commended, as criteria for the judgments that Christians make.

The last chapter of *Christ and the Moral Life* is a constructive statement with normative concerns, and it is in many ways a product of the five previous chapters of critical exposition. It is an exploration or "a sketchy preliminary statement" of a way in which Gustafson's own critical and analytical method can become a basis for the normative tasks of Christian theological ethics. In his own words, the last chapter is "a way of interpreting and explicating Christian moral life regarding particularly some of the differences that faith in Jesus Christ often *does make, can make, and ought to make* in the moral lives of members of the Christian community." [5] Gustafson uses four major categories in this chapter, and not surprisingly, they may be correlated with the three substantive concerns already set forth as being "almost" intrinsic to ethical inquiry. Thus Gustafson speaks of a *perspec-*

---

[5] *Christ and the Moral Life*, p. 240. Two essays that complement the last chapter of *Christ and the Moral Life* are James M. Gustafson, "Moral Discernment in the Christian Life," *Norm and Context in Christian Ethics*, ed. Gene H. Outka and Paul Ramsey (New York: Charles Scribner's Sons, 1968), pp. 17–36, and James M. Gustafson, "Two Approaches to Theological Ethics," *Union Seminary Quarterly Review* (Summer 1968, Vol. XXIII, No. 4), pp. 337–48.

tive or a *posture* in Christian moral life in terms that may be related to his substantive concern for the nature of the good or the
locus of value. His suggestion is that the Christian moral life requires a stance or a fundamental angle of vision which is rooted
in some notion of the nature of the good, and he delineates the
concept of confidence in God as one salient aspect of this perspective. Gustafson then uses two other categories that may be
related to the substantive concern for the nature of the moral
agent. In his brief exposition of what he calls *dispositions* of the
Christian moral self, Gustafson is concerned to delineate those
lasting characteristics or persisting tendencies which can be located in the Christian moral self (his use of the term disposition
is analogous to the classic Roman Catholic category of habit).
Gustafson explicates the virtues of hope and freedom as examples
of the dispositions of the moral agent which are characteristic of
the Christian manner of life. Gustafson also writes of the moral
intentions of the self; his purpose is to draw into focus the fact
that the Christian moral life involves purposive activities. The
intentions of the moral agent, for example, are found in the articulations he makes concerning the governing purposes of his
life; or one may speak of the intentions in a frame of reference
that in some ways corresponds to the concept of the will. In any
event, Gustafson's categories of dispositions and intentions may
both be related to his substantive concern about the nature of
the moral agent.[6] Finally, Gustafson speaks of the ways in which

---

[6] Roughly speaking, Gustafson's distinction between the dispositions
and the intentions of the moral agent corresponds to the Kantian distinction between a phenomenal and noumenal self (the distinction first
appears in *Christ and the Moral Life*, pp. 93 f., in a descriptive sense),
although, unlike Kant, Gustafson wishes to say that the phenomenal
self is as relevant for ethics as the noumenal self. Hence we have as
ethically relevant the self which in its moral action expresses the personal history the agent has accumulated through past associations and
experiences ("caused behavior"). But the self can also be viewed as
free or as being undetermined by its past phenomenal history. Hence
that aspect of the self which is seen to face an undetermined present
and future and which acts out of this freedom to determine that future is also relevant for ethics. Gustafson's main contention, as we un-

Christ is *normative* for the Christian moral life, a category that
may be related to his substantive concern for the criteria, principles, or models used for moral guidance. Gustafson suggests that
Christ functions as a normative reference in terms of one's doctrine of God or in terms of how one interprets or specifies God's
relation to man. Christ also functions as a normative reference,
it is suggested, for the purposes of illuminating what the Christian ought to do (Gustafson has consistently referred to the il-
luminative use of moral principles ever since the Niebuhr *Festschrift* article). Finally, Christ functions as a normative reference
in relation to notions of discipleship, i.e., Gustafson has a normative interest in relating concepts of responsibility or obligation
to Christian ethical life. Thus the last chapter of *Christ and the
Moral Life* may be viewed as a normative effort in Christian ethics which begins with "the nature of the Christian's life in Christ
and its proper expressions in moral conduct." ⁷ Or one may say
that the four categories used in the last chapter of *Christ and the
Moral Life* are an effort to indicate the various ways in which
Christian beliefs have effects on persons.⁸

This brief exposition does not do justice to Gustafson's exposition; it has not even attempted, for example, to indicate the ways
in which Gustafson has interrelated his concepts of perspective,
disposition, intention, and norm. Nor have we attempted to engage Gustafson in conversation about the adequacy of his formulations. But we have tried to make clear in a brief way our own

derstand it, is that both of these aspects of the moral agent are worthy
of a normative interest in theological ethics, and he uses the categories
of disposition and intention in the service of this normative interest.
⁷ The quotation is from "Context Versus Principles: A Misplaced Debate in Christian Ethics," p. 89. The implication of quoting the statement in the context above is that the other base points of Christian
ethics mentioned in that article (social and situational analysis, fundamental theological affirmations, moral principles) would then be reck-
oned with from the perspective of this primary interest. At the same
time, however, these other three base points retain at least a relative
autonomy in Christian ethical discussion.
⁸ See especially the previously mentioned article "Two Approaches to
Theological Ethics."

understanding of Gustafson's intentions. The purpose of this exposition, of course, is to provide a context in which to view the nine essays collected in this modest volume. It is our hope that the perspective we have outlined is not out of accord with Gustafson's intentions and, further, that it is profitable to view other of Gustafson's writings in the light of this perspective. Indeed, we feel that there is a reciprocal effect: the reading of these articles will in some ways be of aid in illuminating the intentions of *Christ and the Moral Life*.

There are a number of limitations to the approach we have taken. There are, of course, other perspectives that would be fruitful as a context for viewing the essays collected here. One could mention as an example the question of the relation of that which is normative (the "ought") to that which is descriptive (the "is"). Just as the movement of *Christ and the Moral Life* is a movement from what claims are made in a descriptive sense about the significance of Christ for the moral life to what claims can or ought to be made (and how they can be explicated) about the significance of Christ for the moral life, so the essays collected in this volume move from descriptive or analytical or critical claims to more normative claims. How are the two different types of claims to be substantiated? Is the "evidence" pertinent for "verifying" the two different types of claims different in kind? Are the descriptive claims rooted in the normative claims, and if so, what is the significance of that fact? The questions provided by this perspective, as well as other perspectives, would be a fruitful point of departure in evaluating the essays collected here. It does not need to be noted that we have not attempted to indicate the ways in which the following essays could be of service to the church as it seeks to fulfill its moral obligations. Nor have we attempted to show how Gustafson's essays could be compared to the statements of others who have written about the mission of the church and its moral responsibilities.

Besides the fact that other perspectives than the one we have delineated would be a fruitful context in which to approach the essays collected in this book, there are two specific shortcomings that can be mentioned about the perspective already outlined. The first is that "moral life" in *Christ and the Moral Life* self-consciously refers to the personal existence of individual men; the moral agent is primarily viewed as the individual agent. But in the essays collected here the predominant concern is with the church as a moral community. While there are shortcomings in making a too easy transition from an individual moral agent to a corporate agent, it is our judgment that more is gained than lost in assuming a direct analogy between the two.[9]

The other basic limitation we mention as a shortcoming of the perspective we have delineated is that it does not focus attention on "the world." Views of man's action in the world, the relation of men to social structures, and their involvement in particular moral issues, are by design not taken into account in *Christ and the Moral Life*. On the other hand, there is a fairly heavy concentration on the first two of these items in these collected essays. Whereas it could be argued that the perspective we have delineated is therefore inadequate for dealing with these essays and that even a direct analogy between the individual and corporate moral agent would not redress this inadequacy, it is our judgment that the obverse is true. We think that the normative concerns embodied in *Christ and the Moral Life* are not only

[9] Gustafson, himself, explicitly makes this analogy in a number of his writings. One of the assumptions that informs this analogy is Gustafson's proclivity for using social and historical categories as common referents for the discipline of theology and the discipline of ethics.

James M. Gustafson, *Treasure in Earthen Vessels: The Church as a Human Community* (New York: Harper & Bros., 1961), 141 pp., is primarily a social analysis of the church. An understated polemic in that book is directed against those who would confine discussion of the church to traditional doctrinal categories, especially insofar as these are timeless and eternal. The reverse, of course, is also true: those who would confine discussion of the church to sociological categories are entering into their own reduction. The last chapter of this book points to the merits of understanding the church as a social and as a historical institution both in theological and sociological frames of reference, i.e., social and historical analysis lend themselves to theological-ethical formulations for both an individual and a corporate moral agent. The analogy, then, is one that is internal to Gustafson's thought. One does not need to draw attention to the fact that the formulations used in *Treasure in Earthen Vessels* are operative in the essays collected here.

relevant to the essays gathered here, but that the focus on the world as seen in these essays is a means of bringing into fuller view the ways in which Gustafson proposes rather tentative normative claims in *Christ and the Moral Life*.

Part Two

The first four essays collected in this volume share the formal characteristic of moving in some way from a description of the world toward proposals about the tasks of the church as a moral community in the world described. In the context of an elaboration of the world a dilemma or problem is then posed with theological-ethical features. Finally, moral-theological proposals are set forth. We shall briefly delineate each of these essays in these terms and then make a few preliminary comments about the moral-theological proposals Gustafson makes in these essays from the perspective we have already set forth.

"Christian Attitudes Toward a Technological Society" delineates the disenchantment of a world pervaded by a spirit of rationality which reduces the elements of mystery and awe in life and concentrates on elements of predictability, calculation, and manipulation. One may make the moral judgment that the fruits of a technological society appear to be both good and evil; technological society is also theologically ambiguous since we deny that God resides in social forms (technology) but affirm that the ordering of life is in God's hands. Thus the dilemma. How are we to respond? In light of the theological affirmation that evil is a corruption of the good, it is affirmed that technological society is a "given" that must be accepted as part of God's ordering of life. This affirmation is correlated with an "ethics of cultural values" in such a way that the Christian response to technological society is delineated in terms of conserving the relative good that exists in it and in making moral discriminations about the relative values which are found in it. What is the significance of these kinds of proposals for the moral agent? Gustafson draws a distinction between the "inner" man and the "outward" world. The inner man is free in the sense that he is not determined by the relative values of the outer world (disposition), and at the same time he is free to responsibly pursue the relative good in the outer world of relative values (intention). However, one may observe that Gustafson urges the merits of freedom in such a way as to avoid discussion of the specific intentions of the moral agent.[10]

This problem is directly related to the problem Gustafson poses in "Patterns of Christian Social Action" which begins with a description of four ways in which the social structure governs the form of man's action (the integration of personal existence, the disciplined exercise of group power, representational witness, and cultural ethos). The forms of Christian social action are also governed by the ways one takes into account the existence of God. In respect to our personal faith in God our action is governed in some ways by qualities of our life which may be said to be a consequence of our beliefs. In respect to the order of the world in which we live our action is governed by our perception of how God orders life. Thus the dilemma. We either claim too much in identifying ourselves with the will of God, or we say too little because we are unable to derive any moral knowledge from our knowledge of God. A potential solution is suggested with the statement that "the inner form of our action, and the form of God's ordering activity meet in concrete action." Still, questions remain about this essay. Does one rely on his dispositions to intuitively guide him in his activities, and if so, how does this work? Or does one rather rely on immediately perceiving the will of God to direct his activities in the world? In both instances the question internal to Gustafson's thought concerns the way in which the dispositional freedom of the moral agent is to be ordered and guided in the world. As we have seen, Gustafson proposes in *Christ and the Moral Life* that the category of the intentional character of the Christian moral agent provides a means of specifying ways in which God's ordering activity and the dis-

---

[10] Criticisms of this type of urging may be found in *Christ and the Moral Life*, pp. 257 f., and they are surely appropriate to Gustafson's own, earlier writings. It can also be noted that in this essay the moral agent's freedom is set in contrast to the ways in which the outer world may determine his actions. One cannot help but think that Gustafson would now clarify the ways in which the outer world may more positively influence the dispositions of the moral agent.

positions of the moral agent meet. On the one hand, since it is assumed that the intention of the moral agent is his own, there is no easy identification of the moral act or the moral agent with the will of God (although, of course, intentions are shaped in some kind of conformity to the agent's beliefs about God). On the other hand, the necessity of formulating and articulating the intentions of the moral agent in the world provide guidance and illumination for the ways in which one expresses his dispositional freedom.

"Authority in Pluralistic Society" is a portrait of large communities in which there is no inclusive object of loyalty or belief. Responsibility is largely conceived as being directed toward a particular constituency within the larger community and in terms of the self-interest of these particular constituencies. Gustafson asserts that social pluralism is an expression of moral pluralism; there are a plurality of claims pertaining to what is right or good. Moreover, there is an absence of any clear and specific way to judge the authenticity of these moral claims. Indeed, different groups authorize the legitimacy of pluralistic society itself in different ways. Hence the loneliness and anxiety of the self-conscious individual is seen as being conditioned in part by the nature of society, and hence the problem. How are we to respond to pluralistic society? The church is to engage in a double task. It is to make viable its proclamation of the provident care of God for his creatures and his ordering of social existence. The church also needs a social ethic to enable its members to make judgments about the relative worth of the relative values of pluralistic society. The role of the church in forming the dispositions and intentions of the individual moral agent and a delineation of the social matrix within which the church may accomplish this function are given attention in later essays.

Whereas the descriptions of the world in these first three essays are in some ways a basis or a context for posing moral-theological problems, the description of the world in "A Theology of Christian Community?" functions chiefly as a foil. The essay begins at the point of an overworked cliché "about modern technological society and the churches' participation in it," i.e., the individual who resides in the private world of person-to-person relationships has no influence in the large, powerful, and public world, and consequently finds himself in a profound state of alienation. Moreover, since the church functions only in the private world of individuals, and then only in a pastoral way, there is, in this cliché, the call for the church to become "secular" as a means of overcoming the gaps. In this essay Gustafson's moral-theological proposals emerge from a description (which is polemically addressed to the cliché) of three aspects of human community (cultural ethos, interpersonal relationships, and institutional power) which are correlated with the purposes of God. It is asserted that God creates, orders (sustains and restrains) and makes possible better qualities of human life in all three aspects of human community. What, then, is the proper response for the Christian from this perspective? The moral agent finds that the patterns of common life which have been correlated to the purposes of God are also patterns for mutual service, responsibility, and obligation. Six implications of the way in which these latter, moral categories may be of aid in viewing the mission of the church in the world are then set forth. We need not enumerate these implications but simply note that it is fruitful to compare the ways in which Gustafson speaks of Christ being normative for Christian moral life in *Christ and the Moral Life* to the ways he uses the categories of mutual service, responsibility, and obligation in this essay.

There are, of course, qualities of worth in these essays which merit attention and which we have not indicated because of the particular ways we have related them to Gustafson's normative proposals in *Christ and the Moral Life*. The same is true of the last five essays which we shall nonetheless relate in preliminary ways to Gustafson's normative proposals by observing that, to a greater or lesser degree, they are all concerned with the beliefs and convictions of the moral agent, his dispositions and/or intentions, the institutional form in which these intentions are embodied, and the ways in which the institutional form of the intentions may be made legitimate. Moreover, we venture the opinion that if we assume some identification between the dispositional character of the individual moral agent (his "caused behavior" and its consequences) and the "disposition" of the corporate moral agent (its "caused behavior" viewed in regard to its social setting) , a greater clarity may be gained about the ways in which Gustafson uses the category of disposition and the ways in which he relates that category to his concept of intention.

"The Church: A Community of Moral Discourse," which assumes that the church's beliefs about God are in some way congruent with its intention to become a moral community, suggests that the intention of the church to become a community of moral discourse can be embodied if it is willing to become acquainted with the moral tradition in which it stands, if it is willing to use fundamental moral principles and convictions in determining the good, and if it is willing to use self-consciously the language of morality, e.g., notions of right and notions of obligation, in nonabstract ways. The intention to become a community of moral discourse, in turn, takes an institutional form insofar as laymen and clergy [11] participate in continuing moral discourse. This continuing moral discourse provides a continuity to deliberation that is as important as the forming of a consensus on any particular issue. The institutionalization of a continuing moral discourse, of course, could be legitimated in a number of ways.

In "Christian Convictions and Christian Action" Gustafson suggests that the category of intention is a way of linking the beliefs or the passionate convictions men have about God with the actions of Christians in the world. Noting that the concept of being deputized by God focuses attention on notions of obligation, Gustafson suggests that the way in which theologians generalize from the rehearsal of the biblical deeds of God makes a difference in the way in which deputyship is conceived. Thus stress is placed on the fact that what Christians believe about God

---

[11] The understanding of the "political" role of the clergy which is mentioned in this article and the next article is more fully delineated in James M. Gustafson, "Political Images of the Ministry," *The Church, the University, and Social Policy,* Vol. II, ed. Kenneth Underwood (Middletown, Conn.: Wesleyan University Press, 1969) , pp. 249–62. See also James M. Gustafson, "The Clergy in the United States," *The Professions in America,* ed. Kenneth S. Lynn and the Editors of *Daedalus* (Boston: Beacon Press, 1969) , pp. 70–90.

provides a foundation for their moral intentions and action. Deputyship is also to be related to the Christian's perception of the world and the way in which it is disposed, hence the intentions of the moral agent are formulated in terms of a deputyship (surely a Christian disposition of sorts in Gustafson's thought) that engages in moral reflection and discourse between identifiable Christian convictions and participation in the occasions and events of the world. The particular ways in which these intentions may be institutionalized and the legitimations of these institutionalizations are assumed.

"The Voluntary Church: A Moral Community" is chiefly concerned to suggest the ethical relevance of the social setting of the voluntary church. The disposition of the church in America is voluntary in the sense that "the will to belong" may be seen as the decisive basis for membership. The will to belong, in turn, is subject to powerful social forces such as neighborhood boundaries, social class, racial selectivity, and national loyalties. It is primarily in this framework that Gustafson evaluates the detriments to and the possibilities for "ethics" in socially heterogeneous and in socially homogeneous churches. Gustafson then explores the problems of "authority and consensus" in light of the fact that the disposition of American churches is also voluntary in the sense that they seek by democratic means to develop a common life among their members. The complex interrelations between the clergy, the laity, and the "norms" of the community, e.g., scripture and tradition, are analyzed as the social matrix for a consensus-forming process, and it is asserted that this process is the key to understanding the vitality of American Christianity. Finally, the theological viability of the voluntary church is substantiated by an examination of the doctrine of the church and the life of the church. If one views the consensus-forming process theologically in terms of beliefs about the *universality* of the presence and power of God, the voluntary church may be accepted as a "practical" (following Kant's use of that word) principle. Hence the church is viewed as the human organization of life through which a Christian moral community can come into existence. A variety of intentions could then be viewed as being in accord with this belief about the universality of the presence and power of God and also as being in accord with the disposition of the church as voluntary.

"Foundations of Ministry" centers attention on the institutionalization of religious leadership in response to the question, What constitutes an adequate institutionalization of the intention and purposes of the Christian faith in our society? The affinities of this article to the perspective we have outlined are so clear as not to require further comment.

"Two Requisites for the American Church: Moral Discourse and Institutional Power" explicitly views the internal life of the church as analogous to the life of the serious moral agent. The church, like the conscientious moral agent, does not just react to events, but is an initiator in the determination of events. The church is enabled to be an initiator insofar as it achieves some clarification of its intentions, purposes, judgments and ends. The church is also like the conscientious moral agent in seeking to achieve its ends, and to fulfill its purposes. Of course, the legitimations of these institutional means are necessary. Again, the affinities of this article are so close to the perspective we have outlined as not to require further comment.

I wish to express my gratitude to Professor Gustafson for his confidence in allowing me to select from his written materials as I have deemed appropriate and for his trust in allowing me to introduce them in my own way. I am keenly aware of the fact that the selection of articles represented in this volume is somewhat arbitrary; the responsibility for this selection and for the Introduction is entirely that of the editor. I wish also to express my thanks to Dr. Connolly C. Gamble, Jr., for facilitating my use of the resources of the Library at Union Theological Seminary in Richmond, Virginia.

Charles M. Swezey
Lexington, Virginia

Part One

The Church in Society

Christian Attitudes Toward a Technological Society

A technological society is a society of disenchantment. We generally assume that disenchantment is a mark of maturity. A child's world is an enchanting world. The patterns of ice and frost on the windows on cold February mornings lead to awesome delight, and give credibility to the wonderful story of Jack Frost. They are not problems to be solved scientifically and objects to be removed by better control of temperature and humidity. Expressions of parental fondness in spontaneous marks of affection are delightfully received at their face value, not phenomena to be interpreted by concepts from depth psychology or explained by statistical correlations between such moments of affection and the lack of tension during the course of one's work in kitchen or in office. The child often delights in the novel, the unexpected, the unanswerable things that take place in the course of his day. He is in a world of enchantment: fear, wonder, awe, delight. Primitive responses are the stuff of his world. Adulthood involves disenchantment of the world. It depreciates the elements of wonder and fear, of delight and awe. Adulthood involves growing rationality.

The technological society is hard put to appreciate enchantment. The artist protests the rationalization of the world with his own forms of deeply personal expression. But men geared to the dominant motifs of a technical age have some difficulty in appreciating the childlikeness of the artist. Technical man's con-

cerns are not directed to simplicity in observation and the pro-
fundity of more primitive expressions of delight or fear. The forest is potential lumber, the mystery of matter is potential energy,
words and ideas are potential means of human persuasion and
manipulation. Persons are functions, potential producers and
consumers. A technological society gets on with its business when
the elements of mystery can be reduced if not eliminated. It seeks
in every possible way to push out the limit beyond which lies the
uncontrollable, the unpredictable, the discontinuities. The elements of childlikeness remain for purposes of leisure; they are
moments of relaxation, of refuge from rationality. They provide
the occasional overtones that keep the melody and theme from
becoming monotonous. At worst, the world of enchantment itself
becomes something we rationally create in order to relieve ourselves from the dominant world of rationality. For the sake of his
participation in a technological society any rational man takes
a vacation, visits the Metropolitan Museum, crowds the highways
on sunny Sunday afternoons, gets a good suntan, reads Shake-
speare and Dostoevski, and drinks martinis. We can rationally in-
duce enchantment, and rationally reduce rationality with a good
stiff drink.

The Rational Spirit

The spirit of disenchantment and rationality is not without
its Christian origins, though other factors are also involved. The
primitive and childlike response of enchantment seems to imply
the excessive holiness of created things. Wonder and awe are the
responses of persons who seem to believe that there is an irreducible sanctity to nature. To profane this sanctity is to abuse
it; to make the world so awesome is to assume that somehow the
deity resides in things. But we can have a calculating attitude
toward the world because, we are informed by Christian thought,
the world is not God. We can treat the world with intellectual
ruthlessness because it is the realm of the creation, and not the
place in which God resides. The spirit of the child, and often
the spirit of the artist, is akin to that of the primitive man who
believes that an uncontrollable power, mana, resides in birds and
trees, in rocks and volcanoes. The spirit of a technological so-

ciety does not deny that potency exists in these things, but the potency is devoid of the primitive aesthetic-religious significance it has for the simple mind. This is pragmatically justified, for the dreadful consequences assumed to be forthcoming in the profaning of the world do not come. But the attitude of rationality in relation to the created world is theologically justified as well; God and the world are separate. We ought not treat the world with a reverence, awe, and respect properly reserved for God.

Further, in the spirit of much of Protestant life there is an ethical impulse to rationality that has contributed to the development of the technological society. Much of classical and pietistic Protestantism has nurtured what Weber and Ernst Troeltsch have characterized as a "this-worldly asceticism." The self-denial is inward; it is denial of ostentatious display of virtue or abundance, the denial of satisfaction from worldly gain and pleasure. Yet it impels a compulsive duty to busy-ness, to hard work, to disciplined life in the world. As Weber has pointed out, the maxims we all remember from Benjamin Franklin, such as "early to bed and early to rise makes a man healthy, wealthy, and wise," are secularized expressions of what has been the religious duty of man in much of Protestant life. Rationality is a religious duty; the moral life is judged by the virtues that lead to achievement in a technological society. Thus the technological society is not related simply to the secular elements of our social history, but is grounded in religious elements themselves: the treatment of the world as created and not as the abode of the Creator, and the this-worldly asceticism of Protestant life.

The spirit of our technological society is the spirit of rationality. It involves the reduction of elements of mystery, with concentration on elements of predictability, calculation, and manipulation of things and persons. Knowledge has as its end not the inner joy of finding a new harmony of the spheres, but usefulness in the human control of human destiny. Economies, social organization, philanthropies, science, education, welfare governments, concentrations of economic, political, and social power—all these things are based upon the implications of rationality. The ends for which these things work, unfortunately, are not as universal as the spirit that informs them. Calculation and manipulation can serve evil masters and reasonably good ones. They can become expressions of self-interest, of the interest of the nation or a particular social segment of mankind, or presumably can be responsibly used in a more universal loyalty. But the existence of rationality, and its implications in calculation and manipulation of persons and things, informs our society and in turn is nourished by it.

Many of the specific aspects of the society in which we live manifest its spirit. Industrialization, a process beginning perhaps with the lever and culminating for us in automation, manifests man's ability to know how to use elements of nature, energy, and humanity in a productive way. Urbanization as the dominant social pattern in the industrialized world is an expression of the need for concentration of labor force, the division of labor, the complexity of processes needed in industrialization. The benefits and the ills of urban existence are both the creatures of the more fundamental spirit. The more recent concerns for a continued increase in productivity, with its consequent requirements for a revision of our assessments of what we need in order to survive, is a fruit of rationality. The whole process requires that persons be able to entice our consumer habits so that money may circulate more rapidly. Power is required to direct and correlate the processes of a technological society. Social power concentrates itself in large scale social organizations: corporations, trade unions, political parties, governments. The immediate world to which we are related is less and less the raw nature of Divine creation, and more and more the culture created by men. Even the most "natural" of occupations, farming, finds a vast world created by men standing between the farmer and the soil, between the farmer and the animal. Commercial fertilizers supplement manure, milking machines remove the simple pleasure of talking to a cow while draining her milk, tractors replace horses. Man is increasingly dependent upon the world created by men; he is less and less dependent upon the immediacies of raw nature given in creation. Perhaps he is also increasingly separated from those realities which remind him that he is not his own author and does not control his own destiny. Or, perhaps in this regard technological society has simply reduced the little crises that confront man in favor of a great crisis with far greater consequences.

Technological society is a rationalized society. It proceeds on the basis of human ability to know and control the course of events. It enlarges the sphere of our dependence upon the things created by man. It feeds on human ability to calculate the factors involved in any decision and action, and to manipulate these factors so that the consequences sought and predicted by men can be achieved. It is a society that seeks to overcome contingency and create its own novelty. It sets farther off the time and place when man acknowledges his limitations, and in turn acknowledges his dependence upon the Divine.

The Christian's Relationship to Society

How have Christians responded to the rise of a technological society? What have been the characteristics of the attitudes of sensitive religious souls to a "thingified" world? What assessments have been made of the relative goods and evils that have come into our history from man's drive toward rationality?

Christians, like sensitive humanists, have been caught in the moral ambiguities of our modern society. In the main they have not condemned social developments as absolutely demonic, nor have they welcomed them as signs of the appearing of the kingdom of God. Indeed, with reference to modern society Christians have had to face a perennial problem in the history of their moral community. It appears that God has called us to live in a given time and place. What is given is not the creation simply of the generation of the present for whom it is provided. The forms of social organization and technology are not of the making of our generation. They are the present shape of a historical process rooted far into the history of the human race. Just as the primitive church did not choose to come into being in the Roman Empire, and did not choose to have to hammer its convictions out in relation to Gnostic and mystery religions, so we Christians did not choose to face questions thrust upon us by our own society. Rather, we are faced with a given shape of the concrete world, and its own patterns are not always susceptible to the reshaping we might wish to do if we could begin de novo, creating our social world ex nihilo. The givenness of our society must be accepted, at least in general.

Christians have been dubious about how they ought to be related to this given society for at least two major reasons. First, its fruits appear to be both good and evil for man. Men are healthier because of technology; the distribution of food and basic materials for the preservation of life has been more just because of the abundance of things we can now produce. Technology has eased the sheer physical burdens of work so that not all man's energy is consumed by labor; many comforts and pleasures that were limited at one time to a wealthy few are now available to all. Perhaps if our society had reached a crisis in which some either-or decision about its basic goodness or its basic evil had to be made, some of our dubiousness would be removed. But there is no such crisis in the minds of most of us in the middle of American abundance, a relative degree of peace, and a modest amount of excitement. There are no clear grounds for the total rejection of modern social and technical patterns. Thus we have to wrestle with obscurity and ambiguity in our relation to them.

It is not only the presence of immediate signs of both badness and goodness, however, that causes us consternation. It is also the conviction of our faith that this modern world is in some measure ordered by God. Such a conviction is baffling when we look at contemporary events in its light. We deny that God resides in the social forms, or in nature, and thus we can treat these things with some profaneness. But we also affirm that the ordering of life is ultimately in the power of God, and that the world in which we live speaks to us of his sustaining life, and indeed of his redeeming love. Christians face the difficult question of determining at what point the technical and social order has reached such a degree of corruption that it no longer reflects God's order, but must be questioned and perhaps altered, or even destroyed.

Such a determination is more difficult because in God's grace we have been granted an inner freedom from absolute determination by the world in which we live. We are not bound to the contemporary forms of life; we are freed to live within them without their being the final locus of our fears and our hopes.

There is an otherworldliness in the Christian life that gives an emancipation from the immediacies of this world. Yet it impels us to act in this world, for the Lord who has given us the modern world as the place in which we are called to live impels us in both joy and in duty to be responsible to him in this place.

Fortunately, Christians have not been satisfied simply to say that the world is full of ambiguities and, therefore, that all things are equally corrupt and equally good. There are tendencies in this direction in the ethics of Karl Barth, but Barth is by no means the dominant Christian ethicist in the churches. Barth can say, "Trust your own understanding"; he can avoid the level of relative moral discriminations because of his singleness of vision, looking only at the goodness of God. Why is the act of the Christian good? Not because of its moral consequences with reference to the neighbor, but because God is good; because God has redeemed the world, and the Christian knows this. Moral calculation is not an important vocation for Christians; they believe in Jesus Christ. But such a point of view is possible because the Christian who expresses it is not in a systematic conversation with the multiplicity of what is given in the world.

Ambiguity is present, and Christians have wrestled with it. The social gospel movement in American Christianity, often oversimplified as an optimistic humanism, really came into being because of the disorders in an industrialized society. The inner impulse of love and grace was challenged by the external conditions of labor in Massachusetts factories, and life in industrialized and urbanized communities such as New York and Chicago. Washington Gladden, Graham Taylor, Rauschenbusch, and others of our fathers in American Christian social movements were appalled by the human consequences of the technological society of their time. They were not swept up into the glory of its moral possibilities; rather, they were moved by the dislocations that accompanied man's increased power to bring other men under his control. The hope of increased democratization and socialization of centers of power and of the benefits of an industrial economy was tempered by the realization that such benefits would not come apart from a struggle. The movement was a call to action, not a call to allow the certain course of history, either in Spencer's

or Marx's understanding of the certainty, to take its way toward
the finally harmonious society on earth. Each man had to choose
with whom he was to act in order to bring a greater degree of
justice into American society. There were no clean white parties
to join, no certain loyalties to which one could forever be committed. For some, socialism provided the proper answer; for
others, the progressivism of Theodore Roosevelt; for still others,
politics farther to the right. But the motif of hope for historical
achievement was tempered by the motif of consternation at what
man had wrought in the human dislocations of the American
economy and its social order. The technological society appeared
to distort man's humanity, to create hideous situations in which
millworkers and immigrants lived, and to make possible the vast
differentiation between the wealth of the entrepreneurs and the
poverty and uncertainties of the laborers. Action was required,
not theological reflection.

Out of this movement men went in various directions. Some
were called to the work of ameliorating the consequences of social upheaval in settlement houses, social work, and institutional
churches. Others were called to speak for the right of labor to
organize, to condemn the "robber barons" and their power. Others felt that nothing less than a serious reconstruction of the
whole society would be needed. The Word of the Lord seemed to
them, as it did to the dissenting sectarians of seventeenth-century
England, to call for radical socialization of property, and a re-
form of almost every human institution. Technology was accepted; the ordering of it and its implications for humanity had
to be rectified.

Alongside of the pioneer Christian critics of the industrial society stood those Christians who invoked the blessing of the Al-
mighty indiscriminatingly upon the men of power and wealth.
Men like Andrew Carnegie sought to find a moral basis for their
success, and turned to the seemingly natural law of competition
to justify it. They were met half way by clergymen, who assured
them that God was on their side. Bishop William Lawrence of
Massachusetts wrote in 1901 that man could recognize two guiding
principles in his life. First, that it is "his divine mission" to con-
quer Nature, open up her resources, and harness them to his

service." The second is that "in the long run, it is only to the man
of morality that wealth comes," for "Godliness is in league with
riches." [1] Henry Ward Beecher, in the flush of Civil War victory,
spoke with assurance for the industrialized northeastern region of
our country, "We are to have charge of this continent. The South
has been proved, and has been found wanting. She is not worthy
to bear rule. She has lost the scepter of our national government. . . . And this continent is to be from this time forth governed by northern men, with northern ideas, and with a northern
gospel." [2]

Such arrogant assurance that God was on the side of industrialization, particularly as was represented by the Protestant entrepreneurs of this region, is superseded only by the often quoted
remark of one George F. Baer of the Philadelphia and Reading
Railway. "The rights and interests of the laboring man will be
protected and cared for—not by the labor agitators, but by the
Christian men to whom God in his infinite wisdom has given control of the property interests of the country, and upon the successful Management of which so much depends." [3] In spite of suffering
caused by the rapid social change that came with industrialization, and by the boom and bust cycle of the economy, the hand
of God was upon those who gained power in the struggle for
survival.

The Christian in Technological Society

The heirs of the critics, and the heirs of those who saw the
development of the technological society as the inexorable historical realization of the will of God, are both with us today. The
critics have many concerns: they are concerned for the depersonalization that occurs when men become objects to be manip-
ulated by other men of power. They acknowledge the element of
social and economic power that is necessary for the establishment
of any rectification in the social disorder. They are sensitive to

---

[1] Quoted by Sidney Mead, "From Denominationalism to Americanism,"
Journal of Religion, Vol. 36, p. 10.

[2] Ibid., p. 7.

[3] Ibid., p. 11.

the implications of a technological society of abundance in the midst of a world dominated by insufficiencies of almost every kind. Alongside of the critics are those who believe that God willed the free market system by which economy, technology, and society are to be governed. Indeed, the passionate faith in the free market system expressed by its religious defenders is far greater than the working faith of men of social power in this tin god. Alongside of those who maintain a prophetic and critical distance from the current manifestations of rationalization, acknowledging its ambiguity and seeking to be responsible within uncertainty, are those for whom competitiveness is God, and the fruits of the present society are good insofar as they manifest competition and bad insofar as competition has been tempered by other concerns. By almost all the canons of judgment, the responsible critics are worthy of more attention. The believers in a pantheistic God, who no longer resides in nature but in the economy of a technological society, are not.

Among the critics there are important differences. Many of these are along a scale, beginning at one point with rejection of the modern society as a fit society for Christian blessing, and moving in the direction of greater acceptance of this society and its particular structures in mass communications, automation, and other institutions as the "given" within which responsible action occurs.

One pattern of criticism stems from a romantic Christian detachment. T. S. Eliot suggests in *The Idea of a Christian Society* that a Christian society can better be established on an agricultural and piscatorial economy than a modern industrial one. We often have a latent nostalgia for the country, where presumably life was ordered, secure, moral, and good. But such dreams are illusive; even fishing and farming are mechanized. There is no new place to which we can go to establish this Christian society. An important principle underlies this point of view. It is that the *natural* is Christian, and that the natural is close to nature in a double sense. Presumably the Christian and natural life can best occur when the cultural world created by man is minimized, or at least the mechanical aspects of it are minimized. Also there is a *moral* order of nature in the fabric of man and

his relations to other men that can be known and can be actualized historically. The technological society seems to distort
man's true nature. At least it is more difficult for man to become
what he truly is in modern society than it was in some simpler
society.

An acceptance of the view that the society is good which enables man to be what he essentially and truly is, does not lead to
romantic-nostalgia in all its supporters. On the part of the contemporary Roman Catholic social movement an aggressive pattern of ideas and action has been formulated out of which the
modern society can be bent to some extent into the image of the
natural society, the society given in the moral law of nature. An
example can illustrate this response of Christians to the technological society. God's order of nature brings into being human
families. It requires stability within the family; basic physical
and spiritual needs must be met. The family is a moral order,
sacred in its own right as a creation of God. Any social forces
which tend to destroy this order must be evaluated critically. Certainly an industrial society, with urbanization and all the pressures of rapid social change and mobility, makes the actualization
of the true nature of the family difficult. A more stable rural
society provided better conditions within which the proper relation of parents to children, families to other families, and all to
the full order of nature could occur. New conditions require new
directions by implication from the understanding of man's nature. An industrial family needs a living wage; it needs to have
enough money so that its physical and spiritual potentialities can
be realized. The wages of workers, then, must be just. But justice of wage is not measured according to productivity alone, or
according to a determined proportion of the total cost of opera-
tion. Justice is measured according to what the family requires.
How is such justice achieved? In part by the organization of labor so that workers can gain their rightful share. In part by state
family subsidies if necessary. In part by a reorganization of the
society and economy itself in which the interests of all groups
will be rightfully considered. The realization of the natural will
be achieved only by action on the part of Christians, and indeed
the church itself, to bend the forces of our social order to the

right moral pattern that exists in life. The order is essentially good; there is an ontological order that exists and is not destroyed. The Christian response to a contemporary social order is to bring it into such a shape that it more clearly manifests the true order. This requires action.

Christian critics, Catholic and Protestant alike, have been concerned for the existence of a personal society, in which there can be a full flowering of the spiritual and aesthetic aspects of man's nature. For the Catholic a society which does not provide the conditions under which personal existence can flourish is disordered, for the spiritual aspects of man's nature are the distinctive thing about the human species. Catholics object to the "thingification" of man in communism and nineteenth century entrepreneurial capitalism alike. They sometimes object to the use of manipulative devices to extort confessions out of men. They are ill at ease when the sheer preservation of life through labor leaves no time for religious and cultural pursuits. Protestants also view the self as something enchanting—something not to be reduced to the central nervous system and its interactions, or to a thing to be directed by centers of power in the hands of men, no matter under what auspices and by what motivation.

An extreme example of the rationalization of man sets the problem sharply. Religious men are concerned with the success of the motivation manipulators, though the success is not proved, for they wonder how far man's control of other men can go before some rebellion springs up from within. But the Dr. Dichters and the mass communicators are working with peanuts compared with the potential of research in the exploration of the brain. Dr. José Delgado of Yale has continued research in the control of motor activity of monkeys through the implantation of electrodes in their brains. Monkeys, at man's will, can be made to look up, extend their arms, or gag. They can enjoy a delicious banana until stimulated through an electrode, and then suddenly spit it out in disgust. Using the pain and pleasure centers of the monkey's brain, the experimenter can keep him docile, or arouse his ire. Indeed, with electronic devices Dr. Delgado has been able to experiment by remote control.[4] We have learned

---

[4] *Reporter*, May 15, 1958.

that many things that work on monkeys work also on man. In the hands of morally responsible physicians fine things can come about. In the hands of someone else, we invite social chaos and the degeneration of man as this earth has known him. Who controls the panel for remote control?

Christians have asked before such techniques were discovered: What is finally inviolable about man? The depersonalization has taken place in many ways. Relationships with people are segmented in character; we recognize others as the girl who sells us our cigarettes, or the man who delivers the milk. We are led to believe that people are controlling our deepest recesses of response through their use of appealing symbols and images, but we dare not become totally suspicious of being used. If we did we would be paranoid, and the whole fabric of society which rests heavily on common confidence in each other would deteriorate. "No man wants to put on nut #999 until he becomes nut #999," Kermit Eby used to say. The simple mechanization of human energy turned out to be unproductive, so Taylorism with its time and motion studies is not so much in vogue. But out of the new concern came more subtle forms of depersonalization: the ethos of organization man in which, in the name of being persons, we play life's game under rules never brought out into the open.

Christians assume something enchanting, awesome, and irreducible about man. Indeed, his moral integrity and his religious relationships are grounded in the more ineffable aspects of man. The capacity to be morally responsible, to engage in purposive action, assumes a "terminal individual" (J. N. Hartt's phrase), a being not totally conditioned by its relationships, not subject to complete cause-effect analysis, more than the sum of its relationships.

The picture of depersonalization is often overdrawn. Mass producers in factories were found to thrive on the moments of play in lunch hours, and to fit themselves into a status system in their work rooms. Family life, for all the institutions that fulfill its former functions, remains deeply personal, indeed almost exclusively personal. The "meaninglessness" that has been decried ad nauseum appears to be truer for many on the fringes than for those in the mainstream of life. Our Marjorie Morningstars go through their existential quandaries, and settle down fairly happily in the suburbs. Overdrawn or not, depersonalization remains a concern. The Jew Buber, the Christians Brunner and Tillich, and many others see this as a great problem in our time. Maritain seeks a humanistic society in which the fulness of personal existence is possible. Tillich suggests that "the person as a person can preserve himself only by a *partial non-participation in* the objectifying structures of technical society." [5]

For some, the concern for the personal is a flight from the technological society. Churches, out of distrust in the anonymity of existence in "mass" society, find a partial answer in the establishment of intimate cells, or small groups in the congregations. Here one can be oneself; one need not be a "role," or a function. Here grace is made real through the intimacy of personal relationships. Like all Christian responses to a technological society, this is subject to distortions from within. Coziness is no substitute for moral responsibility in human existence. Fellow-feeling is no substitute for the anxiety of having to face hard decisions and to act. Indeed, the romantic memory of the intimate warmth of the small group sometimes appears to be a reconstruction of the pleasures presumably found in the stable, quiet, rural communities, communities which were not as pleasant as we sometimes now think they were. Actually, the church has to confront the question of what Christian community is and is not in an urban society. Some have answered that it is a personal community. It is the transplantation of the rural church into the city. Others are not so certain. Personal community may simply reinforce the class prejudices of its members, the pleasures of being secure. Indeed, it may, as in Buchmanism, become so concerned about personal sins and personal virtues that it loses touch with the rationalized society in which it lives. Perhaps, though, personal communities can be a place of renewal out of which people move with new faith and moral commitment into their stations in the world.

---

[5] John T. Hutchinson, ed., *Christian Faith and Social Action* (New York: Charles Scribner's Sons, 1953) , p. 151.

How much of the rationalized society does one accept as the place in which he must live and act? How much can one change this structure? Another distinction made by Weber and Troeltsch is helpful here. It is between the ethic of conscience and the ethic of cultural responsibility, or the difference between exemplary prophetism and emissary prophetism. The ethic of conscience would say that the Christian vocation is to witness to a new order of life without worrying too much about relevance and one's responsibility for the preservation of cultural values—like the preservation of democracy against Nazi or Soviet totalitarianism. The ethic of cultural values would say that what is, is partially good. The proper response is to conserve the good that exists against threats of greater evils, to make moral discriminations about the relative values of things in the present order. Some would bear prophetic witness by being examples of the possibilities of a new creation; others, by moving into the established patterns of society and identifying themselves to the extent of being able to effect some small change. The conditions, they would say, under which the Christian life must be lived are set by the world. Take it as it is, act responsibly within it, exert influence and power to change it where you can, and hope in the mercy of God that the consequences will not be too bad.

I would hazard the guess that many Christians have not accepted the existence of *any* moral question in the rationalized world. They do take it, act within it, and hope for the best. But this is different from the prophetic consciousness that impels much of the best in contemporary American Christianity. Christian prophetism accepts certain conditions under which life must be lived and action taken, but it does not accept these conditions without question. It does not accept them as per se the gift of God, or per se the rule of life. The subtlety of Christian ethics of cultural responsibility lies in its acceptance of the relativities of a social order and technology precisely *as relative*. Power exists—physical energy, economic, military and political power, the capacity to order the course of events within limitations in various realms of life including the personal. Accept the conditions, yes. But all power exists by the power of God; all power is responsible to God; all power is potentially an expression of the divine purpose. Social and personal power, in whatever its rationalized forms, is not in itself good or ultimate. It is something to which Christians must be relatively related while they are absolutely related to God, as Kierkegaard suggests (*Postscript*). There is a rightful relativity to our social structures, our technology, and our economy. Society exists for the sake of man; man and the world exist for the sake of the glory of God. Indeed, these things exist because God has ordered life in such a manner that they come into existence. But their proper existence depends upon their being rightly related to the absolute power and the absolute good, and to the welfare of man. Politics, production of goods, technical discovery, and the whole realm of things made by man are neither to be denied nor embraced without question.

The Christian prophetism we have known, for example in the life and work of Reinhold Niebuhr, has a delicate stance in relation to the world. Man is freed from domination by his society; he does not justify himself according to its norms and standards, but is justified by what God has done for man in Jesus Christ. In his inward freedom man can accept both his own moral ambiguity and the moral ambiguity of the world in which he lives. But his inward freedom gives him freedom to act, taking responsibility without assuming absolute responsibility (which is in the hand of God). Indeed, as Luther, Calvin, Bonhoeffer, Barth, Maurice, and others have helped us to see, God calls us to witness to his power and grace in a concrete world.

The rationalized world is our world in this generation. Its physical scope now extends beyond the limits of the earth. If it is the work of the devil, the devil has created a thing that is awesome and wonderful to behold. If it is the immediate work of God, it is terribly incomplete and deformed. If it is the work of man alone, why did he not do better? How did he manage to do so well? The delight in being human is that we must wrestle with the question of what is our right relation to technological society, in very specific forms. Our right relation is complex, for we are related not only to the world, but to God who has ordered and redeemed it and us.

Patterns of Christian Social Action

The form of Christian action is governed by the social structure within which action takes place. There is a limited number of socially given patterns through which members of the Christian community can exert influence and act in any given society. The form of action is also governed by the existence of the person in Christian faith. There are qualities of life which are consequent upon belief in God, faith in God, that affect the action of the Christian. These are never fully specifiable, but faith affects the style and stance of the moral actor, and in turn the form of his action. The form of action is also understood to have some relation to God's action, to the divine initiative, and to the divine ordering of life. Christians presume that life exists within a framework created, if not redeemed by God, and that action in the realm of the social is not unrelated to the power and order of God.

Dispute among Christians is far greater on the second two points of reference, that is, the meaning of our faith for our action and the meaning of God's existence and action for our action, than on the first—the more empirically verifiable given pattern. Let us examine in greater detail these three: the form of action as governed by the social structure; the form of action as governed by personal faith; and the form of action as governed by God's objective action.

Four Patterns of Action

Christian action takes place within a social sphere. It is action through patterns of human relationships which are relatively set by the contemporary social structure. Any effect upon the order of society comes about through engagement with that order itself. Christians cannot create de novo the optimum conditions for the exertion of influence or the determination of a course of events. Thus while we seek to become self-conscious about the possible patterns of action, and seek to find ways in which our social witness can become more effective, our plans are generally limited to an exercise of present available structures. There are four that seem to me important for Christian action in the age of technology.

First, Christians are members of more than one socially defined community. We are always members of the Christian community and other communities; we are never exclusively members of the Christian community. We are, in a descriptive sense, engaged in social action as Christians in the various communities to which we belong. We act within the more intimate relationships of family and friendship groups. But we are also participants in political parties, management of the mass communications, labor unions, and other groups. In a sense the bridge between the church and other social organizations is already built. It is true that not all important persons in the powerful organizations are serious about their church loyalty, and indeed they may have no Christian loyalty at all. It may also be true that not many persons with strong loyalty to Jesus Christ are in important positions in our society. But there are more persons who join these communities in their own lives than the churches have learned to work with effectively.

The bridge for Christian action does not exist simply by virtue of multiple memberships, one of which is in the church. Membership can be a very external relationship. But one assumes that there is an integrity to the personal existence of most people in which their various loyalties are drawn together and through which loyalties have an impact upon each other. The purposes to which one is committed in one community must find some satisfactory relationship to the purposes to which one is committed in another community. The various centers of loyalty find their own ordering in the character of personal existence. This integration of personal existence is one way in which the Christian community can affect other communities.

Pastors and analysts of contemporary Christianity are prone to understand this, though they see more clearly the ways in which loyalties to the values and purposes of American big business or American suburban culture creep into the life of the church, than they do the possibility of the same process being a means of Christian action in the world. We are perplexed when church boards of trustees incorporate either the sales ethos or the balance-the-budget ethos of American business culture in the life of the church. We dislike having church decisions, which normatively ought to be made in the light of Christ's lordship, being made in the light of the lordship of the budget or of effective fund raising methods. We recognize the integration of the personal existence of these laymen, but deplore that its center is not Jesus Christ.

The fact that this integration exists to some extent marks a possibility for more self-conscious Christian action. There is much evidence that what men believe about God seems to have little implication for their responsibilities in society. Such evidence cautions us against assuming that the transformation of the technical society will take place automatically by enlarging our church memberships, or even by holding religious revival meetings of one sort and another. But the task of the church, with reference to Christian action, becomes clearer. We must help the laymen who are in the church and in positions of social responsibility to interpret their responsibility in the light of the gospel. The meanings, values, and purposes which appear to be the center of their personal integrity must be brought under the scrutiny of the gospel. Their responsibilities in society must be interpreted in the light of the possibilities and limitations of man as these are understood in our Christian heritage. The church must aid them in seeing moral dimensions in their concrete areas of social power, out of which they can exercise more responsible action. The task of the church is not to tell them what they ought to do in specificity, but to enable them to see possibilities of moral value, and pitfalls of temptation in what they are doing and what they can do. The church cannot claim that moral certainty is forthcoming from centering the layman's personal existence in Jesus Christ; it can claim that there are implications for all human action that come from one's faith. The Christian community can help its members understand what some of these implications are, and thus have some impact upon their action in the social structure.

In this respect, we can see the importance of the doctrine of Christian vocation. It needs to be somewhat redefined in relation to current popular usage. Many more romantic interpreters of this doctrine understand it in terms of the possibilities of self-realization that come in one's work. They seek to find ways of making one's work "meaningful," and in effect exhilarating. While this is a worthy aim, and not to be denied, it does not exhaust the potential of understanding our place of responsibility as a place of Christian action. The place of one's action is a place in which one can responsibly exercise social power out of gratitude and obedience to God. Christians have positions of social responsibility. The social structure involves us in social power. We need to understand the possibilities of this, to take seriously in the church the moral seriousness of many of our laymen, and to find ways of more effective action through the common participation in Christian and other communities.

A second means of action governed by the social structure is the exercise of power through socially disciplined blocs or groups. We have come to use the words "countervailing power" since Professor Galbraith renamed an old idea: that is, the domination of a particular power group in the society must be met by the emergence of a group which checks and balances the power of the first group. Or in the manner of Prof. David Truman, we might understand the social process as competition among groups primarily dedicated to their self-interest, and hope that out of this competitive process will come a safe pattern of social balance. But social action through the disciplined exercise of economic or political power is virtually impossible for the church.

The difficulty is particularly clear in the case of Protestantism, for American Protestantism is radically democratized. The laity believe that the church has no right to speak apart from the consensus of its members; that moral authority for the church resides in its general will. If an issue arises around which there is lay consensus, Protestants have demonstrated remarkable political realism. The story of the Anti-Saloon League as the pressure organization for dominantly Protestant interests is a case in point. But issues are few and far between around which such fervent unity can be evoked, and such issues are almost predestined to be oversimplifications of a much more complex moral problem. The clearest issue in our society is desegregation. Boycotts and sit-ins have proved effective but the numbers of participants remains small. If Protestantism is to see that social discipline is necessary for the exercise of social power, its will to action may be paralyzed by this vision. But the churches do not need to become social power blocs in order to affect social power blocs.

Protestants and others can agree on certain relative social values to be achieved. The interests of a morally healthier society can be met in one decade by encouraging the growth of industrial unions; in another it can be met by encouraging legislation to make unions more responsible. Protestant members of unions, political parties, producers' associations, and other organizations can exercise influence in the course that these power groups take. We can learn from Roman Catholic programs in this regard. The Catholic labor schools and organizations such as American Catholic Trade Unionists have had an impact on the whole for the social well-being of the nation, without much aggrandizement of benefits for the church itself. We need not encourage Protestant blocs within pressure groups, though tactically such may be necessary on some occasions. But we can encourage responsible participation in voluntary organizations and pressure groups. The groups exist; they function in our social structure. They will exercise social power with or without any self-conscious Christian participation in them. Our membership in such groups is a possible means of action on our part as Christians.

More limited in its immediate effects on the exercise of social power is the representational witness of Christians as Christians on particular issues. Even a technological society such as ours still pays some attention to the statements of a religious community, based upon the reflection of the best minds of that community. We have not become so totally secularized that testimony on crucial issues—as Christians—is completely ineffective. City governments pay some attention to the reflections and judgments of the Christian clergy, not out of respect for the votes the clergy controls, but out of at least a residual respect for the Christian ethos. Industrialists have been known to invite criticism from Christian thinkers out of deference to the moral perspective that they represent. The members of the World Order Conference in Cleveland were under no illusion that their statement on Red China would immediately change the course of foreign policy. But the statement was a courageous one, and at least informed the policy makers that there were moral grounds for a policy at variance with the one now exercised.

Many factors go into the effectiveness of the representational witness of the church. They differ from time to time and place to place. Our growing realism about social power has led the church to place less significance in this method of social action. Students are not passing many resolutions. Local clergy associations are more adept at influencing public matters through quiet work than they once were. But the testimony of Christian conscience need not be blocked by a recognition of its limitations in the exercise of power. Indeed, testimony of Christian conscience that is coupled with *a sustained involvement* in the patterns that effect public welfare can carry an important measure of weight in the processes of social action. The courage to commit oneself to print about a matter of public dispute is not to be ignored. Intelligent and informed testimony from the Christian community is not totally ineffective by any means. Like other communities, this one can and ought to speak for its convictions.

Finally, we are involved in the shifting general moral climate of our society. While it is hard to locate the moral consensus of our society, we all seem to feel that it exists. Sometimes it is called the collective consciousness, sometimes the spirit of the times, sometimes by other names. But whatever it is called, we seem to understand that the moral climate of the United States is different now than it was in the latter part of the nineteenth century. We can be even more specific. Four years ago the student generation seemed to be "beat," to be without cause and commitment, to be "other directed." Now students are participating in sit-ins and Peace Corps programs; we have a new student climate. Statistical verification of such impressions is virtually impossible, but we are nonetheless convinced that they are largely true. Further we are convinced that moral concern affects behavior; that the social fabric of our society in part depends upon the general moral climate is something on which conservatives and liberals all agree.

Christians cannot afford to lose sight of the importance of this nebulous but powerful force. Other groups in our society are deliberately engaged in an effort to affect the moral climate. The famous Dr. Dichter was once reported to suggest that the growth of the economy depended in part upon the change in the moral approval given to thrift and self-denial. The redefinition of what man needs to be comfortably human is going on all the time. The mood of isolationism is fostered by groups dedicated to isolationist principles; the mood of fear of government growth is fostered by those dedicated to libertarian principles. Again, our realism about social power has sometimes led to fixing our attention upon the clearly defined centers of social power, and ignoring the significance of the moral climate. This climate may set certain limits beyond which the society will not allow policy to go. It may affect the specific goals and policies of private and public agencies and institutions. To be engaged in affecting the moral consensus is a given possibility.

In describing the forms of action that are governed by the social structure, we have not said anything that is very distinctively Christian. Christians simply ought to note what are the socially effective ways in which all persons act, and through which all communities of loyalty affect the structure of society and its processes. There is nothing so unique about Christian action that it can bypass these given patterns of life.

Basic Components of Christian Acts

Christian action always involves the fact of the existence of God. The sphere of reality for Christian action includes the reality of God. This was well put by Dietrich Bonhoeffer: "The reality of God disclosed itself only by setting me entirely in the reality of the world; but there I find the reality of the world already, always sustained, accepted, and reconciled in the reality of God." [1] The reality of God has a twofold significance for Christian action: (1) the personal life of the Christian actor as he lives in faith, and (2) the order of the world in which Christians live and act. More can be said concretely about the importance of the personal existence of Christian actors in the light of the reality of God, than can be said about the implications for the objective order of society.

The form of Christian action is governed by the Christian's faith in God, who has revealed himself in Jesus Christ. The precise act of the Christian does not find its pattern out of faith alone, but action is informed by faith. Some of the common consequences of life in faith can be drawn. These consequences, though inward in character, affect our basic stance in relation to our society.

Christian action is action in hope. It partakes of a "cosmic optimism," not in the sense that the expectations of a historical society of righteousness are to be realized, but in the knowledge that finally the destiny, context, and end of Christian action is in the hands of God. Frustration and bafflement by the complexities of a social order or process of social change are not overwhelming. Christian action rests in a certainty of goal which will be realized. It is grounded in a reality that orders social change, and finally will redeem it. Hope is generated in the belief that God's power limits the morally adverse consequences of human action; indeed that within the divine providence the actions of men can be brought into an order that finally fulfills the divine purpose. Christians face the future without despair, for the openness of the future in God's future. We can "strain forward to what lies ahead," with an ultimate assurance in the victory of the power of resurrection. Social processes that seem erratic and contingent in our sight are not outside the power of God's created and redeeming order. Hope makes us affirmative; we acknowledge pos-

---

[1] *Ethik*, p. 61; Charles West's translation in his book *Communism and the Theologians* (Philadelphia: Westminster Press, 1958), p. 334.

sibility as well as limitation, capacity for new order in life as well as conviction about corrupt order. Hope is one of the fruits of God's spirit that informs the action of Christians.

Christian action is action in freedom. The freedom of Christian action is not only the freedom of all action, that is the possibility of innovating a course of events in the total social process. It is an inward freedom from self-concern and fear, from bondage to legalistic requirements and to the precise expectations of others as the basis of our salvation and self-esteem. Christian action in inward freedom is action out of trust in the goodness and mercy of God. It is action out of gratitude for the gift of God's mercy and goodness. It is the possibility freely to give oneself in action—to give oneself in obedience to God and to the social needs around us.

The consequences of Christian freedom for Christian action are several. We can be free to accept the world in all of its relativities. Responsible action can take place within the immediate sphere of responsibility, for we know that we are not finally to be judged by the perfection or imperfection of the course of events consequent upon our action. We can be objective about the relative claims of groups within our society, for we are not finally bound to an ideology about the supremacy of one group over another. Freedom gives us "distance" from our social responsibilities out of which comes better perspective on what is possible and what is necessary. Yet freedom enables us to be engaged without the expectation of perfection. It is a condition for courage, for taking moral risks. In Christian freedom we can be *realistic* about the means of responsible action. We are not ashamed to use the forms of action governed by the given social structure simply because they are not the creation of Christians out of love.

The freedom of the Christian moves him into the specific realm of action. His trust in God compels him to be identified with others, to become morally serious about his actions. Freedom enables the Christian to have a proper self-estimation; to expect not too much, to be open to new life and new possibilities.

Christian action is action in humility. The humility of Christian action is not abject annihilation of the possibility of responsible action. Rather it is humility that comes from the *acknowledgment* of God's prior power, prior order, and prior gift, out of which action comes. It is humility which recognizes that God can use a broken reed, in spite of its brokenness. Humility is a function of thankfulness: thankfulness that God has called man to places in which he can exercise his holy freedom in care for men. Humility is also a function of self-understanding: an understanding that accepts the limitations of the self in knowledge, in capacity for disinterestedness, in capacity for love and service. It is the humility that acknowledges the *brokenness* of the reed that God in his power uses. Humility makes no great claims for action; it requires neither honor nor reward. It colors Christian action.

Christian action is action in love. Love is an inward principle and order of Christian life. Love acknowledges the freedom of the other. Love ministers and does not rule; its authority lies in its power and not in its claim to power. Action in love avoids the imperial majesty of the ruler, the one who claims for his action some sacred authority. Love seeks the good in concrete ways within the realm of the possible. Love is both motivation and form in Christian action. It is an impulsive power which embraces the good of man and society with a measure of indiscrimination, without regard to status ascribed by the human order of values. Yet it is the form of discrimination, seeking the fitting action appropriate to the increment of goodness and order within the given possibilities.

Hope, freedom, humility, and love are all gifts, given in faith on the manward side and given in God's grace on the Godward side. They are the form of action that comes in the personal existence of the members of the Christian community. They are the fruits of trust, the inward form of Christian action. The *outward* pattern of this inward form is not absolutely determined by life in trust. The inner form finds appropriate outward expression in the context of given possibilities in the society. The form of existence in faith is one among several governing factors in Christian action. It is never to be taken for granted as habits upon which we can rely. The form of personal existence is a gift of the Holy Spirit of God; it is perhaps most reliable when it is least relied upon, when the believer acknowledges a divine agent of action who acts through man in Christ. It is what one can dimly discern and inadequately describe in the confession that "it is not I, but Christ living in me."

Christian Action and God's Action

It is easier to define something of the personal implications of belief in God for our action than it is to determine an external order that God orders, or at least wills. We are hard put to say that a technological society is in accord with God's order at one point or another. We are hard put to say that it is out of God's order at any particular point. Yet Christians are pressed to affirm that there is power, purpose, and structure which is *out there,* which exists not only in the minds and hearts of men but has an objective existence. Christians are pressed to say that the requirements of social morality are governed not only by an inward form of life, but by an objective moral order.

But we are perennially plagued with what more can be said than the acknowledgment of an objective reality and order with its own *thereness.* The *simple confession* that a moral power, purpose, and structure exists gives us no *knowledge* that is of use in our moral actions. Even some of our favorite words sound empty when we seek to draw implications from them for our action. We can say that God is righteous, and that any human order ought to partake of the righteousness of God. But from righteousness to the use of time for purposes of public information on CBS television is a long way, and the path is not clear. Acknowledgment of the righteousness of God has an impact upon the form of our personal existence, but its significance for the proper external ordering of society is not so evident. Troeltsch understood this problem to be inherent in any Christian ethics that grounded itself in the biblical witness alone, and believed that Christian ethics could become social ethics (in the sense of saying anything about the right order of society for a particular time and place) only by borrowing concepts from the natural law tradition.

Christians *have defined* the meaning of the objective moral order, as given by God, and presumably as an order in which God is acting in various ways. The great tradition of natural law has provided one basis for making judgments about what ought to be on the basis of what really, essentially, is the right order of society. For example, from Plato we have learned that justice is essentially a harmonious relationship among the interdependent orders of being. Within the self it is the harmonious relationship and right ordering of passions to intellect, for instance, according to their order of being. In society a pattern is historically required which participates in an order that essentially exists. Or we may use the notion of justice as referring to retribution for actions which disorder the society. Or it may mean a relatively equitable distribution of power and of things in order to preserve order. Whatever its meaning, it appears that justice is required not because some of us are inwardly disposed to be just, but because an order of life cannot continue without justice.

For some generations now, however, we have been acutely sensitive to the historically relative content that concepts like justice and equality have. We are prone to go in two directions from this sensitivity. Either we deny that they are useful concepts because they are so formal in character, or we find them to be *operationally useful* and do not ask what their grounding is in some created order of being. We may say that the *idea* of justice helps to preserve some order in history and society without identifying a particular just order with God's order or with God's presence in human action.

Some Christians have sought to use the idea of the kingdom of God as a pattern for the order of society. We were "kingdom builders" until our theological and social sophistication removed this option from us. Now perhaps we want to say that signs of the appearing of the kingdom ought to be manifest among us, or that there ought to be a foretaste of the kingdom. But we still have a rather formal principle on our hands. Walter Rauschenbusch had more courage than some of us; he dared to risk a content definition of the kingdom and its requirements. It was democratization. Democratization required greater equalization of power and the benefits of a growing economy. From the notion of democratization one could design specific goals, strategy, and tactics for social life. The objective rulership of God required a more democratic order in family, state, education, and economic life.

The New England Puritan Christians also gave some specification to the order of society. The sovereignty of God was to be exercised in church and civil commonwealth. This meant more than pious acknowledgment of a higher law and higher authority, though it meant these. It meant taking the law of the Bible seriously, for the Bible was a reliable revelation not only of what God had done for man, but of what God required human society to be. Further they infused elements of the natural law tradition into their ordering of the civil commonwealth. Since our historical sophistication removes the possibility of literal truth in the Bible, and the application of this truth to a new age, the Bible appears to be of limited value in guiding our understanding of what God orders.

Christians in all times have believed that God is love, and that from this being of God there is an imperative to be loving. Thus we seek an order in which love is given maximum fulfillment. Love is the law of life in a double sense: in the sense of imperative to be obeyed, and in the sense of the ultimate reality or possibility inherent within human life. But we are always faced with the definition of operational implications from love which pertain more specifically to our time and place and the possibilities of achievements that reside there. Love as mutuality is more a possibility in society than love as self-sacrifice, though the former must always stand under the judgment of the latter. Or we derive principles with less authority than the universal law of love and with more potential for realization in the specific situation.

For other Christians what is required is a life of following after Jesus Christ. Some believe this means nonresistance to evil; some believe this means nonviolent resistance to evil. The second group are more socially responsible with reference to achievable purposes than the former. For some this means conformation to an inner spirit of Jesus Christ, so that the witness is that of suffering humility, and finally death itself.

For still others, Christians cannot make significant calculations about the appropriate or inappropriate order on the basis of any moral knowledge. The life of Christian action becomes virtually an intuitive reaction to a particular situation in the sure knowledge that our action is good because God is good. Calculations and discriminations always involve sin; they are always for specific values which are not universal, for the good of a nation, or of a culture. This pattern of thinking seems to deny the importance of social values, the significance of an "ethic of cultural values."

In seeking to know how Christian action ought to be governed by the divine action and the divine order, we are in what is to me the most difficult problem in Christian action. We are in the perilous position of having to say something, but knowing that almost anything we say is either claiming too much, or is saying not enough. It is either claiming too much for our particular actions to say that they follow the pattern of God's objective action, or it is saying that we know so little about what God's ordering activity is that no moral knowledge comes from our knowledge of God. If we accept a call to Christian action in a technological or any other age, however, we must be discriminating, judicious, and informed. We need insight, principles for the interpretation of our actions, and the courage to risk stands on matters which are ultimately highly relative, but presently of great importance.

Perhaps the form of Christian personal existence, the inner form of our action, and the form of God's ordering activity meet in our concrete action. We can risk our relative judgments and actions, accept responsibility for the place in which we are called to act, because inwardly we know the grace and mercy of God which gives us hope, freedom, courage, humility, and love. We can act in the light of our best knowledge derived from various sources about what is objectively required because we affirm that the ultimate agent of all action, the Lord of all life, is revealed in Jesus Christ. The meaning of Jesus Christ is clearer with reference to the inner form of our action than the outer form of our action. Yet it is the same Lord. The God whom we can inwardly trust is the God who outwardly orders life. He calls us in a technological age to be responsible actors in a given structure and process of life.

Authority in
a Pluralistic
Society

Communist societies can be traced in a large part back to the
writings of Karl Marx and his followers. The democratic revolutions were seeded to a significant extent by the social philosophers
of the Enlightenment. Islamic societies have their Qur'an. But the
contemporary pluralistic society has no clear ideological or philosophical roots. It was not planned by a utopian thinker; no one
wrote a philosophical program for it. It does not have a doctrine
of being to sustain its order as the Aristotelian-Thomistic ontology
supported pre-Reformation European society. If, in America, one
might point to the philosophies of William James and John
Dewey as expressing something of the assumptions of a pluralistic
society, one can hardly believe that their writings have influenced
the cultures of many other nations that are rapidly being trans-
formed from homogeneous, and relatively simple societies to heterogeneous and complex ones. Indeed, if some citation of the forces
that brought the contemporary pluralistic societies into being is
to be made, an ideology would be less prominent than rapid
transportation and communication, human migrations, industrialization and the search for markets, propaganda techniques, and
secularization. And clearly there are no biblical texts to which
one might turn for explicit authorization of the complex patterns
of a contemporary society; even more clearly, no theologian has
given us a blueprint. Indeed, the theological and philosophical
reflection about pluralistic societies is usually inductive from a

fait accompli; the existence of these societies precedes the formulation of a doctrine of them.

Before issues of authority and responsibility are addressed, some specification of the usage of the term "pluralistic society" is needed. Clearly the term refers to certain basic trends in the modern world, and not to some pure state of affairs. Indeed, if taken literally, there is virtually a contradiction within the term, for complete pluralism would give one many different societies. Pluralism refers in ordinary usage to a differentiation of groups within some larger minimal loyalty. Thus we call a society "pluralistic" when there exists within one national community a great diversity of competing centers of loyalty, competing systems of beliefs, competing cultural values. Many modern societies are characterized by religious pluralism—in India for example, one has a Hindu majority with significant minorities of Muslims, Protestant Christians, Orthodox Christians, Roman Catholic Christians, Parsees, and primitive animists. In most nations of the cultural West, one has Protestants, Roman Catholics, Jews, Orthodox Christians, agnostics and militant atheists, and anti-religious Marxists. In addition to religious pluralism there are other competing centers of loyalty—political ideologies (more finely drawn in the multi-party nations of Europe than two party United States), economic ideologies, vaguely defined but real communities of diverse morals, and interest groups (labor, farmers, management).

Together with the diversity of loyalties, beliefs, and cultural values, there exists a high degree of institutional differentiation, of specialization of social and economic functions. The decline of the open marketplace for the sale of the farmer's produce is symbolic of this. Between the farmer-producer and the urban consumer one finds, among other institutions, a cooperative marketing organization, a food processing industry (preserving, packaging), a wholesale distribution and sales organization, an advertising agency, the retail store, and finally the consumer. While these diverse functions do not create mutually exclusive groups, they do create a diversity of interest-groups with competing aspirations and desires.

The political structure of pluralistic societies tends to be democratic. While nondemocratic nations have the specialization of labor, and the institutional differentiation that characterizes all industrial societies, they severely limit the diversity of beliefs, loyalties and values. Political, economic, educational and police power are concentrated, and used to enforce a certain order among groups which might compete with one another under the conditions of civil and political liberties. Furthermore, they seek to impose a unifying ideology which demands the supreme loyalty of all the members of the nation.

Authority and Responsibility

Given the evidence that existence of pluralistic societies precedes in time and in fact any major doctrines about them, it is well to continue in the vein of social analysis. The notion of "responsibility" can be taken as the correlate of the notion of "authority." Thus one can ask the question, "To whom (a person, or a group, or an institution) do individual persons, or particular groups feel responsible?" And one can ask, "For what do they feel responsible?"

The answers to these questions would be instructive. In the advanced secularization of the Western world one is not likely to hear many persons or groups acknowledge, "We are responsible to the living Lord, Jesus Christ." In the religious pluralism of many modern nations, one is hardly more likely to hear "We are responsible to God, the one beyond the many." Indeed, the problem of authority in pluralistic societies can be stated in one way as follows: Various subcommunities and groups in society have no common object of loyalty, no universal being whom they acknowledge, no "higher law" that they recognize, to which all of them are responsible. To affirm that "there is no authority except from God, and those that exist have been instituted by God," is meaningless to most groups and persons. If there is a statement such as "One nation, under God . . ." in a pledge of allegiance, the religious reference is either part of the rote liturgical language, or the "God" who is acknowledged is more unknown than the one referred to in Paul's speech on the Areopagus. The reference to God may have a social utility that is theologically false; that is, it might give a comforting assurance that God is the protector of the particular nation. But it has no moral significance, for there is little or no consciousness of what responsibility under the divine authority might connote for the actions of men. Contemporary pluralistic societies, then, are characterized by the absence of acknowledgment of any single authorizing person or agent, to whom the actions of men and groups are responsible.

"To whom are you responsible?" is generally answered by the leaders of various groups as if the question meant "what persons have authorized you to exercise power?" Thus the leader of the trade union feels responsible to the "constituency" that has elected him to office, and before whom he must render an account of his work if he expects to be reelected. Responsibility to a constituency generally means responsibility to the *self-interest* of the constituency; to doing what the members of the group believe to be most beneficial to them. Thus the leader of the labor union is charged with improving the lot of the workers, without primary regard to the consequences of his activity for consumers or other groups. There is usually no loyalty or principle that is acknowledged among labor unions that transcends their own view of their immediate interests, to which leaders can appeal to justify considering the interest of the "national community," not to mention the universal human community. Leaders of other groups in pluralistic societies are in similar situations. Corporation managers feel responsible primarily to the organization and its investors, etc.

The absence of an object of universal loyalty and authority in turn begins to answer the question, "For what are you responsible?" as the above suggests. The leader is responsible *for* the interests of the group *to* whom he is responsible. He views his task to be the pursuit of the good as it is defined by the constituency that authorizes him, and delegates power to him. The leader of a nation might appear to be in a position to acknowledge a wider constituency, and thus a more inclusive loyalty. He is authorized to pursue the national interest, rather than the interests of the Protestant community, the working class, or the intellectuals. Yet in pluralistic societies he tends to define his responsibility *for* the nation in terms of balancing the various interests of groups with diverse ideologies, and diverse desires.

The way in which he can effectively remain in power is defined in part by the social and cultural pluralism. Any expression of his responsibility for the good of the whole nation must be exercised in such a way that it gives minimum offense to the various sub-communities, and minimum damage to their own definitions of what is the good for them. Religions seem to have a peculiar status in this regard, particularly in the United States; a President needs a Protestant pastor, a Roman Catholic archbishop, a Jewish rabbi, and in recognition of the growth of a constituency in American society, an Orthodox metropolitan to pray at his inauguration. He cannot afford seriously to slight any of them. In the sphere of economic policy, while he may have more sympathy for labor than for capitalists, he wants to avoid giving the impression that he is against the business man. And even if the leader of a nation might have a sense of his responsibility for more than the national interest because of a more inclusive loyalty, he cannot win support for a particular policy apart from appealing to more limited interests.

The civil law tends to become the most universal authority and inclusive object of loyalty in a pluralistic society. It is the law of the land that authorizes the exercise of various forms of social power in order to limit the actions of competing groups. All persons and groups are responsible to the civil law, and the persons and institutions authorized to enforce it. Separate interest groups are permitted freely to pursue their ends within the limits set by the law. This is particularly true in American society, where the citizens think of the state and its functions primarily in negative terms. The law does not authorize political parties, nor does it authorize churches and professional organizations. These are authorized by the free agents who gather around a common loyalty to seek to pursue a common end. But the law does define the points at which this free pursuit must be limited, for the rights of other groups to pursue their interests and ends might be transgressed without such definition. The state is responsible for the national interest, understood largely in terms of responsibility to maintain a minimum of overt conflict between groups, to prevent violence and destruction of property in the pursuit of divergent purposes. Labor unions can pursue their interests through the industrial strike; their right to do so is guaranteed by law. Such laws came into being because apart from such a guarantee the power of management was without a balance. But in the pursuit of its interests, labor is limited in its means and techniques by laws and court orders. The police power intervenes when physical violence begins, or when property is destroyed.

Similarly, the civil law defines the limitations within which a particular ideological group must keep in propagating its beliefs. Religious groups cannot engage in physical coercion in order to gain members, or to retain members. Threats of violence or extortion cannot be practiced in order to force men into submission to the will of a political party, or a group that represents a particular ideology. The *ideology* of white racial supremacy, for example, cannot be ruled to be illegal, for pluralistic societies tolerate a great latitude in the freedom of beliefs, and have difficulty in enforcing their convictions even when they assert that a particular belief is "subversive" to the national interest. But when the believers in the doctrine of white supremacy engage in the violent coercion of nonwhites in accordance with their convictions, the civil law exercises its restraining power. All groups are responsible to the law, and to those authorized to enforce the law. The law provides the clearest statement of the social and cultural consensus present in a pluralistic society, for it is an agency of responsibility *for* the inclusive national community. It is the highest authority.

As heterogeneity of values, beliefs, religions, and interests increases in modern society, the law takes on significantly different social functions. For example, the cultural homogeneity of the Scandinavian countries provides a common substance of tradition that has never existed in a land populated by immigrants from many nations and believers of many religious convictions. The national churches of these countries have remained established in a large part because the law of the land represented a cultural consensus, undisturbed by competing religious and secular ideologies. The amendment of the laws pertaining to religious life came only with the introduction of religious pluralism, and the secular ideologies. Under the conditions of increasing cultural heterogeneity, new legal arrangements were necessary to protect the rights of minorities, and to maintain order within a rapidly changing society. No one questioned seriously the right of a theological faculty to exist in a state university until religious and ideological pluralism emerged in a previously homogeneous cultural and religious community. Now the question is raised; and one of its implications is a possible revision of the law, and of the function of the law. The critics of establishment are in fact saying that the function of the law in a pluralistic society is not to authorize a particular religion, or a particular type of theological faculty, but to guarantee that no legal preferences are made. The responsibility of the law for the whole national community with its varieties of denominations and churches, and its unbelievers, requires a revision of all forms of legally preferred status.

Thus, if one proceeds to analyze pluralistic societies in terms of responsibility "to whom" and "for what," a picture begins to emerge. Its outlines point to the absence of any clear, inclusive object of loyalty, belief, and value beyond the multiple interests, desires, and convictions of various groups within the society. Responsibility is generally conceived of in terms of responsibility *to* a constituency *for* its interests and ends. Authorization comes from people, responsibility is for those who grant authority. The affirmation of divine authorization is meaningless to most men and groups. Insofar as there is a more inclusive source of authority, it is the civil law, which in turn tends to become the protector of the rights of all competing groups, and the regulator of the limits beyond which they cannot go in pursuing their beliefs and goals. Whereas once cultural homogeneity, the existence of a substantial ethos, sustained many phases of a society, the introduction of diverse morals, values, beliefs, and ideologies creates issues unanticipated in other times and places. New groups and institutions emerge, rendering obsolete a sociology of *triplex order* derived from the Bible. And no simple proclamation that all men and institutions are responsible to God, who has authorized them, and who ultimately governs them, will in itself resolve the tensions and dilemmas of pluralistic societies.

Authority and the Claims to Legitimacy

To continue in the vein of social analysis, the question of authority can be addressed in another manner as follows: To what do persons and groups in pluralistic societies turn in order to claim legitimacy for their words and deeds? Questions of this order can be answered with reference to many things, and on various levels. Indeed, such inquiry can become the game of the introductory student of philosophy, who is enthralled by the Socratic spirit: "Why did you vote for him?" "Because I wanted to." "Why did you want to?" "Because he is a good man." "What constitutes goodness, and how do you know he is good?" etc., etc. Nevertheless, it can fruitfully demonstrate that the problem of authority in pluralistic societies can be stated in the following way: Various subcommunities and groups in society make radically different and often contradictory claims to legitimacy for what they say and what they do. Social pluralism is an expression of moral pluralism, a pluralism of claims pertaining to what is right, and what is good. Every group in society has some purpose, function or utility, whether overtly expressed or not, and implicit in this is a claim that is moral in character. There may not appear to be any moral justification for a circle of heroin users, but for those who belong one might assume that the use and effects of heroin give a certain pleasant release from the normal states of consciousness. That is good, as they see it. Or the implicit claim may be that since conventional society forbids the use of heroin, the morally serious thing to do is engage in rebellion against convention. In any case, one might investigate the claims to legitimacy of a circle of heroin users, and find at some point a value proposed to substantiate their existence.

The diversity of religious groups in a society can be used to illustrate the variety of claims to legitimacy. Roman Catholics, Orthodox Christians, and various Protestant groups coexist in many modern societies. Each might be provoked to give some reasons for its right to exist. Each might claim that it is the most adequate institutional embodiment of the common Christian truth and tradition. Since each community is certain that it is more adequate as an expression of the faith than the other two are, and since there is no supreme court of judgment in the human society that can decide between the claims of each, it is necessary to tolerate religious diversity. The realm of ultimate claims to legitimacy is one that the pluralistic society studiously avoids, as long as the competing claims do not lead to civil strife. But one finds in turn that diverse religious communities then reinforce their right to exist with the legitimacy granted by the pluralism itself. That is to say, each has a right to exist and propagate itself because they all live in a free pluralistic society. If the tolerance of diverse claims to truth and legitimacy runs counter to a dogmatic conviction of a particular religious group, in turn it finds reasons for making legitimate its self-imposed limitations on the drive to become the single religious community. To pursue the domination that is inherently its right, for example, might lead to greater evil than good in the present situation; therefore, the presence of error is to be tolerated.

Many groups in heterogeneous societies claim a right to exist because they are socially useful. The Polish Falcons, an organization of immigrants from Poland in the United States, has a right to exist because it reinforces the sense of ethnic identity and the perpetuation of Polish cultural influences in a culture in which Polish people are a minority. The Order of Vasa, a comparable organization of Swedish immigrants, makes a similar claim. A war veterans organization claims authorization from the assumption that men who have served in a war together have in common many things—their patriotism, their memories, their economic needs, and their simple need for companionship. An organization to guard against the infringement of civil liberties and civil rights believes that it sustains the cornerstone of a free society. An organization to ferret out all persons who might be sympathetic with any ideas that are remotely related to those held by Karl Marx believes that the free society is best sustained by restricting the civil liberties of communists and any other persons of whom its members choose to be suspicious. Thus a pluralistic society is characterized by the absence of any clear and specific way to judge the authenticity of claims to legitimacy. It avoids having to adjudicate between bases of authorization, except where these violate some clear tenet of the civil law.

Indeed, many enthusiastic proponents of pluralism make a virtue out of this by believing that it is healthy for a society to have groups with competing and contradictory claims to authority. The health presumably comes from two effects of this competition. One is the contributions of "partial truths" that each might make to the total body politic; if they are allowed to make their claims side by side men can choose between them, or some more universal truth might grow out of them. The other is the manner in which competition between moral claims in a dynamic pluralistic society keeps any particular group from coming to supremacy. If various groups have equal rights to exist, even though in a state of competition and potential conflict, they have the presumed beneficial effect of checking and balancing each other's claims to truth, and goodness, and rightness.

Some Fundamental Assumptions of Pluralistic Societies

We have already asserted that pluralistic societies come into being without a self-consciousness that they are distinctive in any sense. Men have not found it necessary to believe in pluralistic societies in order to live in pluralistic societies. There is no clear and explicit dogmatic foundation for them to which men swear allegiance, or confess in some national liturgical rite. There is no pluralistic party line, no blueprint or long-range program developed by believing "pluralists" to give guidance to the actions of men from day to day. The closest one comes to a dogmatic foundation lies in the statements that guarantee the rights and freedoms of men and groups in the constitutions of free democratic societies. In the United States the charter documents—the Declaration of Independence and particularly the preamble to the Constitution and its Bill of Rights—seem to distill the dogma of a free pluralistic society. Yet even these assumed a greater homogeneity of the national community than actually is the case at the present time.

When some philosopher seeks to define the grounds upon which a pluralistic society can rest, as have such persons as J. Maritain and Horace Kallen, he is immediately challenged for his reductionism, and indeed his "monism"! If the foundation that he affirms is to deny that there are ultimate truths and values, he is attacked by those who believe that this is itself a false dogma. Skeptical secularism might become a dogma that seeks to suppress "truth." If the foundation that he affirms is the existence of a universal human nature that has a variety of institutional expressions, but as such deserves respect, he might be attacked by those who believe that any attempt to define a universal human nature is foolish, and always pours some "sectarian" content into its mold. To affirm a particular view of natural law, or human nature is to prejudge what a society ought to become. Thus pluralism is compounded—there are many different assumptions that have the effect of enabling men to live in pluralistic societies. Men conceive of the authorization of pluralistic societies in different ways, just as they conceive of the authorization of particular groups within such societies in different ways. Some of these explicit and implicit assumptions can be briefly noted.

An evolutionary naturalism might be the ground upon which men appear to have confidence in pluralistic societies. The human species in its social forms, as in its biological form, can be conceived of in terms of a body struggling for survival in changing conditions and environments. In order to maintain social existence, the body social must engage in experimentation, using this and that religious system in order to make a satisfactory adjustment, this and that political belief, this and that economic ideology. In the competition among ideologies and groups, the body social will find that manner which best enhances and sustains human existence. Or, it will find ways to tolerate a diversity of group life in order that the needs of some men may be met in one way and the needs of others in another way. In any case, pluralistic societies are a phase of man's adaptation to the changing conditions under which he lives.

A religious conviction about the ordering, the sustaining activity of God in his creation might sustain pluralistic societies. God has created man with certain requirements for the continuity, preservation, and fulfillment of earthly existence. There are ordinances of God which set the direction in which societies go, set the limits of their diversity and their activity, fulfilling the temporal requirements for human existence. In this direction, and within these limitations, there are many possibilities for variation in the realm of belief, of social organization, of value preferences. Judgments can be made about the greater and lesser adequacy of diverse norms, but no historical norms are to be equated with God's order. Nevertheless the sustaining activity of God prevents pluralism from becoming chaos even when conflict among ideologies and groups takes place. Pluralism need not create an ultimate anxiety, because there is one Lord who limits the folly of man, and turns his mistakes into good.

A religiously grounded conviction about man might be the foundation upon which a normative theory of pluralism is built. Since man is finite, there are bound to be diverse understandings of the purposes and principles of human society. The claim for a universally valid set of beliefs, or social forms is a claim to overcome the limitations set by being creature and not creator. Further, since finite man is also sinful man, various competing ideologies and interests are necessary to check man's ruthless thirst for power and domination. No one man, no one group, is to be trusted to formulate an order of human society that is unlimited in its applicability in time and space. The theologically informed view of man might be taken one more step. Since this finite and sinful man has been given knowledge of God's care for him in creation and redemption, he has a positive freedom which keeps him from being bound to a particular set of social conventions, or humanly defined beliefs. Men are free to be diverse; groups are free to pursue different patterns of human life, as long as certain rudimentary considerations grounded in our knowledge of God's care for man are met. Pluralism is not merely an expression of man's natural freedom in such a view, but it is an expression of the assurance that God cares for man, and thus is free to find those modes and expressions of life that are suitable to his diverse needs and responsibilities.

The Single One in Pluralistic Societies

The situation of the self-conscious individual in highly pluralistic societies is, to say the least, anxiety producing. He is confronted with several possibilities for his existence; he can select (or drift into) one of many moral communities. He hears the competing claims of diverse groups, and is tempted by the almost universal appeal to self-interest as the authority for his life's goals. Pluralistic societies give the impression to the self-conscious single one that all values are equal, and that one's choices are merely a matter of one's social conditioning, or one's emotional preferences. Sustained unifying traditions are few, and those that exist are without any particular authority. There are few large communities to reinforce one's own values, and if one is found, it is contradicted by the existence of other communities holding other values. Flexibility and change are more visible than order and stability. Pluralistic societies seem to require a high degree of tolerance of ambiguity and diversity.

In an extremely pluralistic society, demands are made upon the self with which many persons are unable to cope. Many men cannot tolerate the existence of such heterogeneity; they cannot make intelligent and discriminating choices; they cannot hold fast to a sustaining tradition in the face of the criticisms made of it from other socially respectable points of view. A secularistic point of view declares that God is dead, and the proclamation of his death confirms the suspicions that lurk in the consciousness; or if made with scientific authority the proclamation has the effect of killing God for many men marginal to the religious community. Not every man is prepared to defend that in which he believes in the face of intelligent opposition, socially permitted. The single one becomes the lonely one; and in loneliness seeks some company to reinforce his being.

Thus the way is often paved for the fanatical attachment to some belief or pattern of life, or some communal loyalty that fills the emptiness of uncertainty. Without certainty that there is any one to whom man is responsible, one who sustains the moral order, men are prone to attach themselves to a finite cause with the passion of a lover. If the existence of civil liberties makes possible a continual debate about justice and order, and a sustained critical attack on the status quo, some men flee as if back into the womb into a fanatical cause that proclaims the sanctity of their petty beliefs, and the heresy of all others. In the absence of personal faith in a living God, to whom one owes absolute loyalty, and in whom one can have absolute confidence, men are prone to find objects of authority, secular ideologies, in which they place confidence. But these ideologies and temporal communities often acknowledge no higher law than their own interests, and thus become dangerous and disastrous pseudo-authorities, usurping the place of God in the consciousness of men. Thus pluralistic societies offer the possibility for fanatical flights from what appears to be a confusing complexity of groups, ideologies, and values into the false absolutization of a single center of human loyalty. One sees this, for example, in the John Birch Society in the United States.

A Double Task for the Church

The church has at least two words to address to the problem of authority in pluralistic societies. First, it proclaims the reality, the existence, of the living Lord, who has brought all things into being, and whose provident care sustains and preserves life from human self-destruction. It proclaims that all human communities stand under the divine authority, and are judged by it, that they are finite and corrupted, and not worthy of final loyalty and trust. It proclaims God's care for every single one, as well as his ordination of social existence, and thus provides the ground of faith and hope and love out of which pluralism can be tolerated, and indeed, become a fruitful historical mode of common life. It proclaims that all men are responsible *to God, for* the neighbor, near and distant.

Second, the church needs to maintain a continuing interpretation and critique of the various movements that claim men's loyalties. It needs to maintain a running dialogue with the social options of a pluralistic society, so that those who acknowledge God can make discriminating choices and responses to the options given by society. Too often the Christian community has waited until one ideology, one social option has accrued massive power, and its demonic character has become unambiguously visible, before it begins to acknowledge a critical social task. The church needs a genuine social ethic, one that does not limit itself to alternative exegeses of Romans 13, nor limit itself to the affirmation of the existence of a divine order somewhere. It needs a social ethic that helps its members discern between the more and the less worthy centers of loyalty, the more and the less worthy secular perspectives on politics and economic life; the more and the less trustworthy cultural values. It needs a social ethic that helps its members judge the claims to legitimacy that groups and movements make. A sustained interpretation and critique of society is required from the perspective of the community that acknowledges that there is no authority except from God.

A Theology
of Christian
Community

One of the more overworked clichés about modern technological society and the churches' participation in it runs something like this: In modern society there is a profound alienation of man from the structures of work, politics and other aspects of life. The large, powerful public world seems to be managed by a few persons in the seats of power or, in the view of analysts, appears to be running not only itself, but the persons who are supposed to manage it. The church has no way of influencing these centers of real power in the world, for in an age of secularization its moral authority is no longer recognized, and it lacks the modes of exercise of social power to become a significant pressure group to countermand the tendencies that appear to be against its understanding of what life is meant to be. Alongside this powerful ordered public world is the private world of person-to-person relationships, of family life and of individual existence. It is in this sphere that some of the protests against the alienation from the structured world take place—the rebellions of youth or the efforts to achieve some compensating meaningful life by concentrating on family activities. The church, we are told, has become functional with reference only to this private sphere. And even here its role has become supportive, therapeutic, pastoral and even idolatrous, for it functions to give religious sanctions to a culturally defined pattern of life that is itself not sufficiently subjected to theological and moral criticism.

The effect of much persuasive writing in this vein, by Marxists and existentialists, by theologians and some Christian sociologists, by world-renowned philosophers and street-corner culture critics, has been to create a mood of hostility toward the church even on the part of many who continue to call themselves Christians. The churches are seen to be part of the problem of alienation, for they have been attending to institutional demands for self-preservation, to cheap piety and to concern only for the private sphere, none of which rectifies in the least the moral impotence of institutional Christianity. They represent religion, and this, on testimony from anti-bourgeois theologians, is bad. The avant-garde Christians then call us to a radical secularity that, we are to assume, overcomes the embarrassment of church life which seems to be merely pious and private in its morality, and institutional in its demands. Secularity also presumably overcomes the distance between Christian faith and the centers of power where things that really matter for the life of man are taking place.

Certain assumptions that inform this perspective need to be brought under serious question. They are both sociological-historical and theological in character. We may ask whether the division between the private and the public, the personal and the structural is not too sharply drawn, and whether significant relations do not exist between them. We may also ask, from a social-psychological perspective, where the person-forming communities are going to be in a program of action that looks with disdain upon the church and other "private" spheres. What is to shape the mind and the spirit of the person who is told to be completely identified with the "world"? What is to provide a center of his own personal existence which informs his involvement in the secular order when religion, as a historical movement influencing persons and cultures, is apparently not to be cultivated? What kind of sociological assumptions lie behind the view that Christians can be socially more effective by involvement in secular institutions, since it is through these that history is being shaped, while at the same time the institutions and the religious culture that shape the Christians are judged to be increasingly useless? Where, also, is the positive place of custom and of cultural values, of ethos, in this critical material? In the anti-bourgeois stance, have critics failed to distinguish between false and suppressive moral customs and order, on the one hand, and the positive significance of cultural morality, on the other? There appear to be theological assumptions lurking in this kind of social analysis as well. They are many, and they do not form a single consistent school. Insofar as the social analysis moves to the cultivation of an existentialist mood, one wonders if God is not seen primarily in terms of the accepter of persons, the lord who wills meaningful moments of self-realization in personal terms, rather than the sovereign ruler of depersonalized institutions as well. The mission of the church becomes focused too exclusively on the personal and interpersonal. Insofar as the social analysis leads to the glorification of the secular world, where Christ's lordship is presumably being worked out, one wonders whether that world, like the church, is not also deeply corrupted by unfaith and rebellion against God. One wonders sometimes whether we cannot rely upon Christ's presence and lordship in the church, and indeed through religion, as much as we can rely upon his lordship being exercised through social crisis and social change. There is a stress on secularity without adequate delineation of how Christians judge the secular. Insofar as the social analysis separates the realm of the personal from the impersonal, but assumes that God's dominion is pressing in upon both, one wonders whether there is not the legacy of a Lutheran theology and a Brunner theology that sees God doing work with persons through the gospel with his right hand and with institutions through the law with his left hand, in such a way that these are spatially or chronologically separated. The realms of redemption and of preservation become sharply divided, with a different ethic for each.

Debate over adequate social analysis and over theological assumptions has some significant effects on the actual life of the Christian community within the wider community. Our institutional forms and activities are guided in part by the sociological perceptions and theological interpretations. The establishment of "coffeehouses" as places of ministry adjacent to college campuses in the United States, for example, is informed often by crypto-sociological assumptions about what the actual situation of society is—one in which students are alienated and thus must be ministered to in terms of that alienation. It is also informed by crypto-theologies, believing that God's grace is known in the intimacies of coffee, poetry and jazz, and is not known in the course of study or in the world of "establishment." The founding of centers for discussion of vocational and political problems may assume not only that the churches as they are now organized cannot effectively speak to the world, but also that conversation about the world without embarrassing reference to theological conviction and to religious interest is the way in which God (if there is a God) works in the modern world. I do not intend to be overly critical of the new forms of witness and mission, since for both sociological and theological reasons I affirm their place in the life of the church. As many have noted, the traditional routinized activities of institutional churches in all parts of the world also certainly rest upon sociological perceptions and theological interpretations that have to be brought under question.

It is my intention in the main body of this essay to suggest an interpretation of community, based upon sociological and theological perspectives, which I hope is more adequate to sources of truth and of insight than some perspectives that are currently in vogue or are historically influential in the life of the Christian community.

The Functions of Community in the Light of God's Purposes

What purposes of God are being realized in the existence of men in community? We should have in mind all three aspects of human community: cultural ethos, interpersonal relationship and institutions. My answer to this question hinges on a number of verbs: God creates, sustains, restrains and makes possible better qualities of life through the existence of men in all three aspects of community.[1]

---

[1] This section has clear echoes of the thought of my late colleague and teacher H. Richard Niebuhr, which I readily and gratefully acknowledge, although he would not necessarily have approved of precisely what I have done here.

Common life in various segments of humanity is a means by which God's *creative purposes* bear fruit for men. What is new emerges out of the common life of the old. Human creative achievement takes place within the patterns of life in which persons are related to each other, whether one is thinking of biological procreation, development of new forms of social organization, novel patterns of art and music or scientific and technological developments. Creative work is related to the past in dependence upon it, as well as in rebellion against it. Creative persons are sustained by communities as well as by defending themselves against them. The continuities need to be stressed in an age that is preoccupied with finding discontinuities and with celebrating the novel. Underlying these achievements of men is the potentiality and purpose of newness, or creativity, which is part of God's gracious gift to men in the giving of life. Two examples will make clear how God's creative purposes are achieved through human community.

Newness in human understanding of the physical world is one of the forms of creativity that dazzle the mind. The fresh interpretations we are given, not only of the minutest possible sources of life and energy in the physical world, but also of the relations of the constellations of "universes" to each other, enable men not only to understand the natural world of which they are a part, but also to participate in it with greater intelligence and to master aspects of it for human purposes. Creativity in the world of natural science, however, is not a matter of one person in isolation contemplating introspectively or calculating on the basis of his individual observations. It is a communal enterprise. There is a community of scientists, evoking criticisms and responses from each other, building upon each other's observations and theories, in communication with each other through their own abstract symbols and words. Creativity in perception and understanding, surely in the divine providence a possibility and purpose given by God, is born of intense life in a human community.

Even where the individual appears to "break through" with radical novelty, he is participating in an ongoing community. The rejection or transformation of a traditional pattern in one of the arts, for example, does not come into being as a creative act out of nothing. It takes place as a creative virtuoso responds to the inadequacies of a tradition for the purpose of expressing what he perceives in the world, or what he feels about himself and his world. Novel forms are not de novo forms; they are creative responses to patterns that have been given. The discontinuities can be great, as for example in the development of the twelve-tone scale in music, but nevertheless a community is present—one over against which the new is defined; and quickly a new community is born, developing the fresh pattern. Newness, creativity, comes into being through the existence of common life.

Common life is a means by which God sustains human existence in the world. There is an ordering of existence, changing in its particular forms, to be sure, that provides for the continuity of life. Human life is sustained by the continuities of custom and belief, of values and ideas, as well as by the creative perceptions which alter the traditions of men. The ethical importance of custom and of ethos is an area neglected by many Christian interpreters of society today, probably because a defense of it seems in the West to be a defense of a bourgeois outlook, and many Protestant theologians wish above all to be differentiated from that. Life is sustained by the meaning that one person has for another in friendship and marriage, in pastoral relationship and teaching. It is sustained by the ordering of economic and political power through civil law and through institutions of commerce, police power, trade unions and family. Even when men revolt against a given institution or custom that has sustained them in the past, they seek not the absence of community, but a new community organized by a different institutional form, or by a different set of customary standards. The sustaining power of the tribe is cast aside in the aspiration that the nation will take its place as the formative community. The rigid extrinsic code morality of nineteenth-century tradition is rejected in the hope that a more meaningful morality, intrinsic to man's deepest needs or to his Christian life, will come into being. Sustaining patterns of life deserve a dignity in a Christian interpretation of community that is sometimes overlooked, particularly in a time of revolutions and when individuals find custom and tradition to be so oppressive that authentic human existence is often defined in terms of radical freedom from them.[2]

A part of the sustaining function of community is the restraints that it places on individuals and on other communities. The organized interests of one nation act to restrain the aggressive interests of another. The fighters for justice for those who are oppressed are limited in the means by which their struggle can be executed by the existence of a community that concerns itself for the preservation of civil order. The willful inclinations of the antisocial individual are restrained by the existence of mores and customs, as well as by the civil law and the powers of police enforcement. The personal community of family is not only a pattern in which its members sustain each other physically, mentally, and spiritually, but also one in which limits are set upon the activities of each other by the obligations of its members toward one another and toward the family as a whole.

Through communities the ordering (sustaining and restraining) work of God for the sake of men takes place. New patterns of this work come into being, and older patterns pass away. One of the mistakes of those who define "orders" of creation and preservation is that they often find a kind of revealed positive sociology in the fact that men exist within family and state, as if there were a clear pattern for these institutions ordained by God.

---

[2] A question is implicit here that deserves long and serious study. One gets the impression that much of the Christian social leadership and experimentation is now directed toward those who are alienated from the past and from present communities, and some of it makes for an attitude not just of criticism of "establishment," but of sheer rebellion against establishment as a prime virtue. I do not wish to suggest that particular attention to the depressed and the "outsiders" is not important, but some of it is being given to the neglect of meaningful interpretation of the significance of pattern and order for human beings, and of the ways in which old orders can be reformed to fulfill better the necessary functions of human social life. We seem to be much clearer about the oppressions of custom and institutions that sustain us than we are about their positive functions in the sustaining of human life, and thus about how these patterns themselves can be altered better to fulfill their essential moral purposes.

This, as has often been seen, can lead to a false identification of an existing historical pattern with the divine order, and thus to an uncritical, conservative acceptance of a status quo. We have now properly learned to speak of ordering rather than orders, in the light of the errors of the past. Or to use a different set of words, community can be interpreted functionally, as accomplishing purposes needed for human life. Its particular form or order is to be judged by its effectiveness in fulfilling its morally purposive functions. God sustains and restrains life through the functions of state and family and other institutions, as well as the historical occasions for them that occur through the development of mass public education, through the work of universities and their institutes, through political parties, through labor unions and through international organizations.

Through community, God also makes better qualities of life possible for men. Indeed, while sin is not redeemed by community, God's redemptive love can take particular historical force and form through the relations that persons have with and for each other. Even civil law, as an establishment of new patterns of justice and order in human society, functions to bring new possibilities or qualities of life into being in particular societies. The order of law and the order of society can be the means by which God's love makes possible better existence both for social groups and for individuals.

Community, then, through God's creative use of it, has a high order of theological dignity in a Christian interpretation; it is not merely something oppressive, hostile to authentic life, embodying sin and prejudice. The social mission of the church, in turn, needs to be related to each of these aspects of human community, with each of the aspects of God's purposes in view.

It would be very one-sided, however, to acknowledge that the corrupt, the demonic, the sinful did not also exist in human community. At least since the time of A. Ritschl and W. Rauschenbusch we have come to understand the existence of "kingdom [or perhaps better, realm] of sin." To cite the positive significance of custom and tradition for human community in the economy of God does not imply that custom cannot be perverse and run counter to God's purposes for man. The embedding of racial prejudice within social custom is one case in point. Tradition can also be oppressive, functioning as an idol that prohibits men from responding to the call of God in the openness of the present. To cite the sustaining and even redeeming importance of inter-personal relations, of being for the other person, is not to imply that such relations cannot be demonic and destructive, cannot be the means by which perverse domination of one person over the other takes place, or the means by which inhuman servility of one person under the other is justified. To suggest the positive ethical importance of institutions and civil arrangements in the human community is not to deny the existence of unjust laws, or the magnifying of the effects of human selfishness through the use of economic and social power over workers, or over a nation. Indeed, corruption, perversion, distortion of purpose exist within each of these aspects of human community; human relations are a realm both of sin and of God's creative, ordering and redeem-ing presence. They are constantly under the judgment of the presence of God; they are constantly in need of prophetic criti-cism and reformation; indeed, they also await the full redemp-tion that is to come. But we err if we see only their perversity, or if we fail to give them a high level of dignity in our understand-ing of God's work for men.

Community and Moral Action

These same patterns of God's care for man that are apparent in human community are also the patterns of mutual service, re-sponsibility and obligation within which men are called to moral action. Christians together in the church are particularly called to interpret their existence in community as the location in time and space of their responsibility to God for human society and for other persons. To participate in a cultural ethos, in a moral tradition, is to have responsibility for that ethos and tradition. To be personally related to another is joyfully to serve the other and to be obligated for his well-being. To function as a person within an institution is to see the power of the institution as the means for the upbuilding of humanity and to acknowledge the responsibility of the institution for the preservation of justice, liberty and order in the world. The patterns of common life are patterns of service, responsibility and obligation in a Christian interpretation of community, to God and to men. They are patterns in and through which moral activity takes place. In response to God's goodness man freely and joyfully serves not only individual neighbors, but the common life that binds men together. This is most easily seen in the realm of interpersonal relations. The other is one whom I love, one whose good I can seek, one whose presence I can sustain, one whose despair I can help to overcome, one in whose presence I have delight and joy. Existence in family life makes the details of this clear. In his love, God has given the others to me: wife or husband, and children. In their love for me, the others sustain my life and bring to it joy and delight. In response to the love of God and the love of others, freely given, faithfully given service is an expression of moral action. But service is not confined to the interpersonal.

Participation in a location of responsibility in an institution is also a call to service. Consciousness of the care of God for the human community through government and university, through voluntary associations and political parties, evokes a response of grateful service to others through these institutions. They are the spheres in which freedom, love and concern are expressed. Their own internal structures can be shaped in part by expressions of freely given love and care. They can be shaped in part to be consonant with purposes that express the Christians' response to God's goodness.

Life in community is also life in common responsibility.[3] It is the acceptance of accountability for the shaping of the values and customs that inform much of the unconscious responses and actions of the members of the human community. Community is held together by custom and tradition; good and evil are embedded in custom and tradition; custom and tradition shape the character of persons and institutions so that loyalties and convictions drawn from them inform the responses and actions of persons, even when they are not aware of them. Persons with a

---

[3] For a succinct account of the nature of responsibility, see H. R. Niebuhr, *The Responsible Self* (New York: Harper & Row, 1963).

minimum experience of cultural pluralism within a nation or across national boundaries are conscious of the fact that attitudes, emotive expressions of moral convictions, words and actions often express cultural values different from their own. Part of the pattern of responsibility in community is responsibility for these often inarticulated values, customs and traditions.

The Christian community has the responsibility to articulate and criticize this glue of custom that holds societies together. If tradition and custom regard Negroes or certain castes as inferior and dictate prejudiced attitudes and actions toward such groups, it is the responsibility of the Christian community to engage in the alteration of these forces. If tradition and custom sustain respect for personal liberty and inviolability of conscience against powers that seek to invade and manipulate men, the Christian community has a responsibility to maintain and strengthen these forces. Such forces have in many instances no definite location: there is not always an institution that is dedicated to the cultivation of the evil or the good that is present in an ethos. Yet through instruction, prophetic writing, the nurturing of the minds and spirits of children and other means, the Christian community can exercise influence in shaping the forces that in turn invisibly shape the attitudes, responses and actions of men.

Interpersonal relations are relations of responsibility. They exist not merely as occasions of joyfully given service, and certainly not merely as occasions for self-realization. Faithfulness of one for the other is an aspect of the interpersonal. To be for the person is to be faithful to the other person, to accept responsibility for the well-being of the other. Through interpersonal relations, God cares for the well-being both of the self and of the other. As active persons in these relations, Christians interpret them as occasions of responsibility to God for the care of others. As the promises of the marriage service so vividly suggest, to be related as husband and wife is to be related not only in freely given affection, but to be responsible for each other. Indeed, responsibility for each other is a structure of love, not merely the occasion for love. It is a pattern of service and responsibility. Parents are located in a pattern of responsibility to God for the well-being of their children. Friendship, if it is not confused with mere acquaintance (as it often is in the United States), is not just the enjoyment of each other, taking delight in the presence of each other; it is also the acceptance of responsibility for the needs of each other. To be for the other person is to be responsible for the other person.

The formal and informal patterns of relationships established within institutions and between them are clearly patterns of responsibility. As active agents in institutions, Christians particularly interpret them as centers of power and influence, the conduct of which has moral consequences in the society, and therefore institutions are to be understood in terms of moral responsibility. This responsibility is not a thing, a substance, as it were, that institutions could have. It is rather to be articulated in detailed terms for particular institutions; for the political party, the management of a small business and so forth. Christian interpretation asks certain questions of institutions: For what is this institution responsible? How do its purposes cohere with an informed understanding of the manner and ends of life that Christians believe to be consonant with what God is seeking to say and to do? How can persons in institutions act to give direction to their activities so that the well-being of humanity is sustained and improved by the policies and activities of institutions? In the divine economy, institutions and their relations to each other are patterns of social life in and through which moral responsibility—to God, for the human community—are exercised.

Obligation—a stronger word than responsibility—also enters in. Life in community is life in a structure of moral obligations, of claims upon persons and of claims upon groups. To participate in the community of custom and tradition is to be obligated to God for its rectitude and its nurture, for its continuity insofar as its effects reflect an understanding of what God wills to do for men, and for its alteration insofar as it is a corruption of what God seeks to do and to say. To be sure, the Christian community is in a sense emancipated from cultural ethos; it certainly does not find its final righteousness and justification in its responsibility for the customs and traditions of the society of which it forms a part. Its loyalty to God gives it a position over against custom and tradition, its faith gives it a freedom from bondage to social custom and tradition. But this freedom ought not to imply that the Christian community has no obligation to God for the sustenance and cultivation of those customs and traditions which can be a means of God's governing and edifying work in the world. I have sought to make a case for the positive function of culture in the divine economy; if such a case is made, the Christian community is obligated to God, who rules and upbuilds through culture for the moral quality of that culture.

Mutual obligation is an aspect of interpersonal relations as well. Personal relations, if they are significant, exist over long periods of time and across the boundaries of spatial separation. To be for the other person is to delight in his presence; it is also to be responsible for him, to be obligated to him. In many forms of personal relationship there is a formal rite which not only confirms that two persons will be faithful to each other, but that they are obligated to each other. The marriage service is again an excellent example of this fact. There, a covenant is made between two persons, before God and a congregation of his people which details some of the obligations that exist, by virture not only of the freely given love of one for the other, but of the fact that this love is a faithful and responsible love. As such, it is fitting that there be an articulated, determined detailing of the structure of obligations that both express love and nourish love. Obligation in personal relations is not antithetical to love; it is a form of responsible and faithful love. Marriage is not the only interpersonal relationship in which this is the case.[4]

---

[4] An American is constrained to comment at this point upon the difference between the casual interpersonal relations of his society and the formalized relations of the continent. Friendship and acquaintance have come to mean virtually the same thing for many Americans: there is no sense of being responsible for the other person by virtue of friendship, and no sense of obligation that gives the other a serious claim upon one. There are no little rites that signify a transition in the character of the relationship. By contrast, the mutual consent to move from the polite to familiar form of "you" in more traditional societies symbolizes not only that two persons are at home in each other's company, but that they virtually pledge themselves to a kind of faithfulness to each other which may entail responsibilities and obligations. The interpretation I am giving to interpersonal relationships obviously would place

"Steadfastness" or faithfulness as an aspect of interpersonal relations, with the implied duties and obligations toward each other, is a part of the Old Testament interpretation both of covenant and of love. It is not a nineteenth-century or post-Kantian imposition of extrinsic rules or duties upon persons. It is part of the Christian conviction, born of God's revelation of himself, that informs the church's understanding of relations between persons. In the time of a "new morality" that comes into being under Christian auspices, a morality that smacks of a kind of shallow concern with self-realization, it is perhaps even more important to see the significance of the structure of personal relations as a structure of mutual obligations of persons to each other and for the consequences of their common life.[5]

In the institutional spheres of life, the aspect of obligation is more clearly seen. Institutions have rules and laws which articulate the obligations that persons have toward each other, and the duties that they have toward the institution. But a Christian interpretation is not a mere support of obedience to institutional laws and rules; it is rather an understanding that institutions and those acting in and through them are obligated to God for the conduct of affairs, and thus obligated to the persons and society of which they are a part for the actions and effects of the state, the economy and so forth. Institutions are locations in which man's obligations to God and to other men have a concreteness, a virtually material quality, which expresses man's moral discernment and care. The Christian community is obligated first to God and then to and for the institutions in and through which duties toward God and the neighbors can be carried out.

---

a high value upon such articulations of a "covenant" even if made only in the mutual consent to address each other in the more familiar forms of speech.

[5] One looks in vain for any serious discussion of obligations in the books that often are covered by the appellation "new morality," such as J. A. T. Robinson's chapter, "The New Morality" in *Honest to God*, and Paul Lehmann's *Ethics in a Christian Context* (New York: Harper & Row, 1963). One suspects this is so because obligation suggests law, and law seems to be antithetical to an ethics of grace in which the "divine indicative" has such clear centrality of attention.

Implications for the Mission of Church to Society

Some suggestions about the implications of this interpretation for the work of the church seem to be in order. It is not for me to spell them out in terms of practical programs, but only to indicate stresses and correctives that appear to be required in the present situation.

First, and most obvious, is the need to keep all three aspects of community in view. Those activities of the churches and other agencies that view the Christian concern to be primarily personal obviously tend to neglect the institutional patterns of society. The concern for the personal often leads to a disengagement from the realm of the technical and the impersonal. Indeed, there are theological options that encourage this disengagement by judging the realms of technology, bureaucracy and other forms of organized social and economic power to be virtually demonic, and at least to be detrimental to the ends that the Christian message seems to have in view. It becomes difficult to move from the existential and the personal to the technological and institutional if one's interpretation of modern communities, in theological and sociological terms, places the weight of importance and dignity on the realm of subjectively meaningful existence. The kind of mutual involvement that develops between persons through the impersonal patterns of large-scale social organizations provides, in the light of my interpretation, both for significant, meaningful life, and for moral activity in giving some direction to the course of human events. God's purposes, as discerned in the scripture and in tradition, relate to the historical course of events, and ipso facto to technology, bureaucracy and other aspects of industrial societies that are of crucial importance in our time.

Second, these activities on the part of churches and other agencies that are institution- and "world"-orientated must not lose sight of the importance of the "private" and the personal as spheres that sustain persons in their institutions, and more particularly as places in which there is a formation of outlook and of values that in turn deeply affects the kind of judgments and actions that persons make in their "offices" or institutional responsibilities. The private sphere is not only a place of escape from the pressures of the institutional sphere; it is not only the location of a pastoral and therapeutic concern that can never be ruled out of the purposes of the Christian gospel. It is a place in which are formed the attitudes, reflective moral commitments and motives that persons carry into the institutional and technical world. Choices, moral judgments and actions reflect in part the commitments, loyalties, values, and motivations that are nurtured and reshaped in the sphere of interpersonal existence. If an understanding of community as a process of action within orderly patterns has validity, attention has to be paid to the spheres within which moral habits, character, decisions, indeed, virtues, and their opposites are shaped.

Third, the interpretation given in this essay calls for a far more extensive place for the virtues than popularly exists in Protestant ethics today. Basic selfhood is shaped in the "private" and interpersonal spheres, in the family, the congregation and other centers where the attitudes and values of persons are formed, criticized and in part re-formed. Protestant theology has for too long tended to assume that the language of the "virtues" necessarily implied an uncritical approval of bourgeois attitudes, or suggested that to take the task of shaping the conscience, or of shaping virtues seriously is to live by self-righteousness and law rather than by grace. Indeed, in societies which are undergoing rapid change, with traditional external standards in flux, it is all the more important that the basic loyalties and convictions of persons shall have a measure of stability and clarity, so that their participation in the world may receive direction and purpose.

Fourth, participation in institutions on the part of the members of the Christian community ought to be governed in part by their life of faith, and by purposes, objectives, means of action that reflect the Christian gospel and are informed by the ethical reflection of the community. Life in the church is life revivified by fresh apprehension of God as the sovereign ruler of the world, by renewed dedication to his purposes that is engendered by worshiping him, by informed conscientiousness about the responsibilities and actions in the world that are coherent with the church's understanding of what God seeks to have this world to be. It is in the common life of the church that both intentions and dispositions on the internal, subjective side, and purpose and patterns of life on the external, objective side are to be engendered, fashioned, critically scrutinized and articulated. There is no doubt that the churches as we know them have been remiss in fulfilling this moral function, but we have no other historical social unit within which these functions, in allegiance to Jesus Christ, are performed.

Fifth, culture, or ethos must not be left out of the purview of Christian interpretation and action in society. It is notoriously difficult to influence, since its values and styles are developed by so many different agencies. Protestant churches, and others as well, when they have addressed the problems of culture, have often made sweeping critical attacks about "materialism" rather than finding ways in which to influence the goals and purposes that persons seem to absorb from their milieu. The place that is given to culture in the interpretation offered in this essay calls for a continuous dialogue between the Christian community and other groups, all of which are involved in the shaping of culture. There are signs that this is occurring in the critiques of movies, television, advertising, novels, business ethos and other distillations of culture that have been published under the auspices of Christian churches. Rejection of culture is largely gone as a stance of the Christian community. But apart from persistent critique of it, accompanying our constant involvement in it, we are seriously faced with the temptation to become a new generation of culture Christians, and in our critique of it we often fail in two respects: the faith becomes too readily identified only with the movements of protest against mass culture, and it begins to look as if the Christians had their stakes exclusively in the causes of angry young men; and in our anti-bourgeois sentiments, some of which are in harmony with the claims of the gospel, we are prone to isolate the critical concerns for culture from the daily involvements in it of unexciting, hum-drum mothers, children, clerks, executives, laborers and professional people. Too often Christian critiques of culture are critiques of the Christian cultural élite who, by virtue of their own advanced tastes and training, have separated themselves from the masses whose daily involvement in ordinary affairs God uses and on whom the élites depend.

Finally, we need to find a way in which to reintroduce the idea of obligations and responsibilities without falling into the traps of legalism and heteronomy. These are the traps that ethics is most conscious of today, sometimes at the expense of the right sense of duties and obligations. Indeed, it becomes easy to slip from an antilegalism into an ethic of self-realization in which immediate fulfillment of desires, rather than deepest human needs, is the goal of life. Grace and love drive us from within to become involved in the needs of the neighbor and in the suffering of the world, but under God's sovereign rule we are obligated to take on the burdens of the world as his responsible deputies, even when inner disposition is weak. Life is to find fulfillment in the relations between persons of each sex, but the fulfillment is also one of the duties and obligations that we have toward each other by virtue of these relationships in the divine economy. Faith and love bring us a new sense of freedom, but a pattern of responsibilities and obligations exists to keep that freedom directed toward those things which are helpful and which build up. Neither we nor the world is as "mature" as we are often told, and in the absence of such maturity the necessity of rule and authority under God in determining conduct and activity is indispensable. God's concern for the ordering of human society so that freedom and fulfillment can abound is as much a part of his purposes as is his emancipating men from the bondage of false orders and outdated rules. The interpretation given in this essay calls for more detailed understanding of the church's activity in society in terms of the ordering of institutions and of the duties and obligations of persons at each place of Christian life in the world.

Part Two

Moral Perspectives on the Church

The Church:
A Community
of Moral Discourse

The theme "The Nature of the Church" can be one of the most divisive in Christian thought, making significant communication difficult between Catholic and Protestant, between mainline Protestant and left-wing Protestant. There is a segment of that theme, however, which bridges substantive theological differences. I have chosen to call that segment "the church as a community of moral discourse." It is a normative theme—any discussion of the purpose of the church necessarily is normative. But it is a normative theme that deals with task, or functions of the ministry and the congregations rather than with the theological doctrines of the church and the ministry.

A premise upon which all might agree is that the churches by tradition and vocation bear a responsibility for the morality of the society of which they are a part. In the Roman Catholic Church this responsibility is expressed through the encyclical writing of the popes on social questions, through various programs endorsed by the conferences of bishops, through the specialized activity of Catholic Labor Schools and similar organizations, and through the influence on opinion and action that local parish priests can exert. In the Church of Sweden, a Lutheran Church, a moral responsibility is exercised through conferences and publications on social questions, through a "Christian group" in the parliament, and through public debate in the secular press. In the United States almost all denominations have agencies responsible for research, education, and action on matters of public morality, for example, the Council for Christian Social Action in the United Church of Christ or the Unitarian Universalist Fellowship for Social Justice.

The ways in which religious moral influence can be exerted in America are deeply conditioned by the voluntary character of church life and particularly of Protestant church life. Since no church has an official status in the law and government of the land, there is no legally defined court of religious moral authority to which lawmakers and others can turn for some kind of expert moral judgment on questions of public policy. Since church pronouncements on social questions cannot be supported by the power of a Protestant voting bloc or pressure group, they can easily be discounted by social and political "realists" who are responsive to pressure. Since pastors are no longer surrounded by some aura of moral expertise to which the laity acquiesce, any oracular power they might have had in the past no longer exists. Since questions of social morality involve technical knowledge of the data involved—economics, nuclear weapons, international aid, procedures of social change—the exercise of moral responsibility requires more than a capacity for "moral" argument, and "moral" judgment. The technical knowledge is not readily found among church groups, and thus their influence is often judged to be "uninformed" or "naive." Indeed, by a continuing process of delineating what churches cannot do effectively, one begins to see that what they *can* do is limited.

Without suggesting that churches can *only* be communities of moral discourse, I wish to suggest that this possibility provides a way of responsible activity which is central to any Protestant conception of a voluntary church. By a community of moral discourse I mean *a gathering of people with the explicit intention to survey and critically discuss their personal and social responsibilities in the light of moral convictions about which there is some consensus and to which there is some loyalty*. The effects of such discourse upon the action of the persons involved, and upon the significant issues of social responsibility cannot be predicted in any certain way. The participants are agents or actors who are involved in intricate patterns of social relationships, and who finally decide and act as beings capable of decisions and self-direction. The effects of such discourse upon the actual shape of social events in part depend upon whether persons of eminent social influence share in the conversations. But reliance for exercise of social influence and power upon the lay participants in the religious community is sound. It has precedent in the Christian tradition, and particularly the Protestant tradition where lay participation and consent have been theologically normative. It has particular precedent in the congregational traditions represented by much of American Protestantism. It is also sociologically sound: that is, a major avenue for the exercise of moral consensus rests with the persons who consent to, and are loyal to the moral convictions. It is through their own identity with the values of the community, their incorporations of these values into the determination of their actions, that the values become socially effective.

The minister is a participant in the moral discourse, and what he does is in part determined by the fact that he does not have a clear legal authority to determine what the moral consensus will be. Sidney Mead suggests in his essay "The Rise of the Evangelical Conception of the Ministry in America (1607–1850)" that the relationship between minister and congregation in the American voluntary religious system is really a "political" relationship.[1] The notion is suggestive for our purposes. He cannot be "forced upon his people, without their suffrage and voluntary support" (Lyman Beecher, quoted by Mead) ; yet he is not simply the errand boy of their majority rule. What he ought to be and can be is discussed below.

The Discourse Is Moral

I wish to explicate a view of the congregation or other meeting of the church as a community of *moral* discourse. This is *one* function of the church—not the total purpose, one must reiterate. Religious life in America is shot through with gatherings of people for various purposes: budget decisions, Bible study, prayer,

---

[1] H. R. Niebuhr and D. D. Williams, eds., *The Ministry in Historical Perspectives* (New York: Harper & Bros., 1956) , p. 218.

picnics and fun, etc. Particularly in our time it is my impression that much of the gathering of people together is for some *therapeutic* intention, that is, some kind of religiously sponsored group therapy; or for the sake of "I-Thou" relations in which persons will "get to know each other as persons" in order to overcome alienation, or loneliness, or depersonalization. I wish to distinguish a *moral* intention in the church from a *therapeutic* one without discussion about how they might be related to each other. In moral discourse there are some objective convictions about the nature of the right and the good that are not identified with the existing subjective feelings of people involved; there is a body of conviction or doctrine in the light of which judgments can be made that is acknowledged to be worthy of loyalty whether this body of conviction is internalized or not. In *moral* discourse we are not particularly concerned about whether the participant has some feeling of self-fulfillment, some new sense of well-being in the psyche or the soul. We are concerned with the direction of human activity in the light of an understanding of what is right and wrong, what is better and worse.

Nor is moral discourse simply shop-talk about political problems, or problems of business management, in which one's own capacity for making judgments is broadened and deepened by hearing about the experiences of others who have similar responsibilities. This might be an ingredient in such discourse; indeed, it might even be its starting point. But unless there is a self-consciousness of the existence of some moral convictions that are expressed in a tradition or in moral maxims, or in some other way that exists independently of any particular person's acknowledgment of them, the language and thought of duties and morally viable ends can easily be avoided.

In stressing *moral* discourse, three points of elaboration are important. First, the community and its leaders need to be able to delineate some moral tradition in which they stand. I wish to be generous rather than exclusivistic in delineating a body of moral doctrine, but it is at this point that a more traditional Christian has the most difficulty in empathizing with the radical liberal Protestantism of the Unitarian Universalist societies. For Christian ethics, certainly, the Bible functions as a place in which some delineation of a moral consensus for the churches exists. It suggests some of the reasons why the Christian community takes moral responsibility seriously (a post-ethical question, to use Henry David Aiken's distinctions) .[2] We are obligated to be morally serious because of what God has done for men, what God wills man to be, and God requires life to be. The Bible narrates how a community of Israel came to understand moral responsibility under God—in terms of their actions and historical events, in terms of distillations into moral laws, in terms of abstractions such as justice and righteousness. The Bible delineates the actions and sayings of Jesus Christ, a life that was so faithful and obedient to God that it reveals God's will toward man. The Bible gives us the beginnings of a Christian tradition in which the community expresses in word and deed what manner of life was worthy of the gospel of Christ. The moral discourse in the Christian community takes place in the light of the understanding of what God wills and requires, what God has done and wills that man should do, as these are expressed in the events and the discursive words of the scriptures.

This is not to say that the Bible is a book of rules for moral conduct which merely need to be applied through the processes of moral discourse. Nor is it to say that the Bible is a theoretically consistent document of moral doctrine—it obviously is not. But it is confessionally an authoritative locus of consensus about what the shape and purposes of life in relation to God and to man ought to be. Thus the discourse of our time is discourse in the light of this body of conviction.

Nor is this to say that the only authoritative moral wisdom to be brought into moral discourse is to be found in the Bible. There is no claim in it, and very few have sought to claim since the canon was closed, that moral insight is to be found exclusively in that book. The heritage is more generous than Bible alone. The Christian moral tradition itself developed as this biblical norm was lived and thought out in relation to both the moral ideas and the historical events engaged by Christians under diverse circumstances. Moral discourse takes place in the light of

[2] See H. D. Aiken, *Reason and Conduct* (New York: Knopf, 1962) , pp. 65–87.

88 THE CHURCH AS MORAL DECISION-MAKER

the wisdom and understanding gained from Aristotle and Kant, Joseph Butler and Gandhi, as well. But the conviction needs some shaping, some delineation of what is better and worse moral doctrine which authoritatively but provisionally governs discourse and conduct.

Thus, second, I would briefly elaborate the need for "*ethical discourse*" in the churches.[3] That is, with the richness of heritage, there needs to be some defense on the part of the intellectuals in the religious community of fundamental principles and convictions which help to determine what is "really" good, what is "really" right, what is "really" desirable. The leadership of the community needs to be able to make persuasive arguments for the moral authority of the body of doctrine to which men are loyal, to which they consent. The questions that men have faced in the history of Western ethical thought need constantly to be faced. The determination of what members of the community ought to do, or ought to judge to be right, needs to be clarified by clearly addressing the reasons why one course of action is better than another, one judgment better than another. To introduce the complexity of this level of discourse simply and rapidly, one might say that the community ought to seek the good of the neighbor. This is a part of the consensus of the tradition. But why seek the neighbor's good rather than my own? Why not a principle of self-interest rather than a principle of benevolence? One can see where this leads with just a little intellectual imagination.

I am not suggesting that the church *first of all* is a community of *ethical* discourse—that is, a community of the university or of intellectuals in which the issues of the history of ethical thought are learned and rehearsed. This is necessary, and interesting, and perhaps ought to be engaged in as widely as possible in the life of the church. But it might well be an escape from moral responsibility itself. I wish to affirm that in the church these questions have primarily a practical importance, that is, they enable one to give good reasons for the direction of his activity which is always concrete and historical (or even existen-

---

[3] See ibid.

tial) in character. But here one of the tasks of the minister is introduced: he ought to be better equipped than most in the congregation to provide direction at this critical, intellectual level of discourse. Moral discourse can be discourse about family life or politics; he may not be the expert in these, but he can be the expert in the conversation on questions of "ethics."

The third point I wish to elaborate is the necessity of using *the language* of ethics and morals in the life of the church. There are many practical reasons why this is so, not least of which is the contemporary tendency (perhaps more in mid-stream Protestantism than in radical liberal Protestantism) of the church to be viewed as primarily a therapeutic community. By this I mean simply that if the language of salvation, self-fulfillment, relief from guilt and anxiety, in short the language of what religion can do for you (i.e., your self-interest) dominates, the purpose of the church is askew. The evidences of moral language in the Bible need not be rehearsed; they are at least as prevalent as the words that can be seen to be basically therapeutic. The biblical and Western religious tradition is a religious-*moral* tradition—something that Max Weber's comparative studies certainly substantiate. The language of command and obedience, of responsibility, of good and evil, of right and wrong, better and worse, are part of this language of morals. These words appear to the contemporary ear to be "moralistic"—and this usually triggers a reaction against conservative fundamentalistic legalistic moralism, or pious do-goodism which is so much a part of American life, and the personal lives of many Americans. But religious men in the Christian and Jewish traditions are *moralists*: we are concerned with the *right* ordering of human relationships, we seek the *good* of the neighbor. Moral discourse requires moral language: obviously not exclusively, however, for the *right* ordering of human relationships takes place within a political context (and thus the language of politics), an economic context (and thus the language of economics), and a family context (and thus the language of sociology and psychology). But to speak of political, economic, and family life without self-conscious use of moral language is either to assume the values built into those forms of discourse, or to deny the relevance of ethics.

The language of morality, it needs to be added, is not just the language of abstract ethics. Again, the Bible is generous with instruction. The parable, for one example, is suggestive. Jesus did not engage in discourse (and this is part of the Jewish tradition) in abstract terms, seeking to define the nature and essence of the good, and then to extrapolate from that a direction of conduct. Rather he used the suggestive picture language of the parable, giving the contours of what might be right action through narratives and illustrative accounts. He told a story. A comparable way might occur in present discourse. An illustration of serious moral action under certain conditions might be as persuasive as a rational moral argument. For example, the rehearsal of the Montgomery bus boycott more effectively persuades men of the rightness of nonviolence than an argument from some principle of human nature or divine revelation.

A Community of Moral Discourse

If the voluntary and lay character of the church is taken seriously, not merely as a necessity thrust upon us by our American religious history, but as something intrinsic to our religious tradition and theologically normative, we can properly stress *discourse*. The congregation is a place of speaking and hearing: often this has meant the minister speaking and the people hearing, or the Word of God is the speech and men are the auditors. But those traditions which became the fountainhead of New England religious life generally permitted many of the important ecclesiastical decisions, for example, the evaluation of a candidate for ordination, to be made by the deliberations of the laity. In English Congregationalism a tradition of "church meeting" was maintained for many generations. Such a meeting did not discuss merely the budget and election of officers, but sought to come to consensus through the deliberations of the congregation about what God's will was for this gathering of his people. There was an objective "body of doctrine" upon which I have insisted— the scriptures. But there was a serious effort to find what the content and shape of the activity of the community ought to be in a specific temporal and spatial location through men speaking and hearing each other.

This historical allusion is instructive. With a bit of imagination one can suggest how this heritage can edify our present efforts to be morally responsible as religious communities. There was reliance upon the power of the Holy Spirit to use the conversations of men in order to come to clarity about what God required them to be and to do. To demythologize such an affirmation, we have simply the commonplace observation that discourse and deliberation between informed and morally serious men is more likely to lead to action that is fitting and ethically defensible than are other procedures. But this commonplace is rarely utilized in church life. Rather than rely upon open discourse, and run the risks that are involved in it, most ministers and church leaders select other available options. A common one is reliance upon the persuasive power of personality to bring support to some moral judgment or cause that the minister in his isolation has decided is worthy of loyalty and action. Ministers often are very unwilling to enter discourse; they prefer to come to conclusions without its benefit, and then seek in pulpit or in one-to-one relations to bring men to their own point of view. To use the familiar Weberian terms, in the absence of traditional, or rational-legal authority, and in fear of discourse, ministers take recourse to whatever charismatic powers they may have. Obviously, this sets the minister up as the isolated intellect, assures him of freedom from the anxiety of public alteration of his opinions, and if he is successful feeds his ego-needs. But realism about ourselves as ministers ought to make us see that we need moral discourse as much as any other man.

Another escape from discourse is to assume that if the congregation hears the ministerial wisdom, or even the faithful presentation of the body of doctrine, the individual members will be able to relate this to moral obligations and opportunities by themselves. This presumes that what is said to the congregation is clear, and that its implications for the time and space field of their lives is also clear. But ministerial delusions are fostered in this way. Reference to the experience of southern ministers in the past decade illustrates the point. Several who have been forced from their pastoral charges have reported that they thought they were saying things relevant to race relations for many years by preaching about Christian love, and caring for the neighbor, and they thought the implications were clear to the congregational members. The delusion is clear: suddenly they had to be specific about implications, and realized that no consensus had developed about what was said or what it meant for the life of the people. Again, the moral target was missed.

Clearly, discourse among informed and morally serious men is more likely to find the fitting and responsible judgments and actions than is solo-performance by ministers.

Another dimension of the deliberative process in the moral community is the contribution that persons with specialized talents and training can bring to bear on one another. The minister is rarely the informed man on such a question as the proper zoning for the development of a changing and growing community. But in such a community issue, there are many people who assume that they are experts when in fact they are vigorously pursuing their self-interest, or that of their particular economic or neighborhood group. And there are likely to be persons who are technical experts on the considerations that ought to be brought to bear upon such a question. The dimensions of discourse become clear. A conversation between a technician and an ethically informed minister *alone* suffers from several deficiencies: some considerations of justice that are informed by the self-interest of groups might well miss the attention of two experts precisely because they are not passionately involved in the defense of an interest. Further, the element of persuasion of opinion and conviction that is always a part of moral discourse is shortcut by virtue of the absence of persons who must bear the consequences of action. The consensus between two experts is patently too exclusive. What I am suggesting is evident: churches as communities of moral discourse need to involve the intelligent participation of specialists who can inform each other as their attention is directed to some moral and social policy. The specialization of knowledge makes moral discourse all the more necessary. Churches also need to bring into participation persons who represent varieties of interests, conflicting loyalties and values, so that whatever consensus emerges is informed by the feelings and judgments of various groups. (Here, we need to note the necessity of socially inclusive churches if the deliberative process is to be effective, and I mean inclusion not only of various races, but levels of intellectual achievement, occupations and other factors.)

If moral discourse is deep in the life of a congregation or denomination, the church does not need to rely so heavily upon "pronouncements" as a means of exercising moral influence. Indeed, while statements might well express a moral consensus that is brought into being, they are probably not as persuasive as is the discussion out of which they have emerged. I am suggesting that participation in a serious moral dialogue moving toward consensus is more important than the consensus itself. Max Millikan, in an essay "Inquiry and Policy: The Relation of Knowledge to Action," [4] suggests that the importance of social research for policy makers is not the conclusions of a scientific study, but the argument by which these conclusions are drawn. "The purpose of social science research should be to deepen, broaden, and extend the policy maker's capacity for judgment—not to provide him with answers." [5] So it is with moral discourse. The result of an argument in morals does not provide the answer to which all participants take an oath of allegiance and obey as they do the law. Rather, participation in moral discourse deepens, broadens, and extends men's capacity to make responsible moral judgments.

If the churches see themselves as communities of moral discourse, they might well provide a continuity of deliberation that is much needed in our society. "New occasions teach new duties." True. But there are more new occasions in human existence than there are responsible groups thinking about them in terms of duties and proper ends. Particularly in the splintering of the Protestant community, there is no center for discourse about questions of vast consequence on which Protestant and all other people must make judgments. Here the Roman Catholic Church is instructive. One may not like what Catholics are saying about the population expansion and means for controlling it, but there has at least been a developing moral tradition which faced special and general problems related to this through the

---

[4] Daniel Lerner, ed., *The Human Meaning of the Social Sciences* (New York: Meridian, 1959) , pp. 158–80.

[5] Ibid., p. 167.

years. There is a consensus pertaining to some of the ends to be sought in any policy, and there is some consensus upon the various means that might be used. By contrast Protestant moral discourse is sporadic. If an evil appears to be strong enough, or a moral crisis great enough, then suddenly we are thinking about it just enough to get into the act. Catholics in Japan and elsewhere are the heirs of a process of continuous moral deliberation when they face population growth, and when they see that there are more abortions than live births in that country as a means of control. Protestants might be confused by the conflicting ends sought —smaller population, but more "humane" ways to do it. But mostly they are indignant about high abortion rates. Indeed, Protestant morality has lived too much off of indignation, and not enough on deliberation in relation to ongoing and changing moral obligations. This is true in congregations and in denominations.

In the institutional differentiation of our society, there are few groups that attend primarily to the questions of morality. The church is perhaps one of the chief ones; others might be voluntary associations for particular moral purposes. Universities seem tragically to have resigned the function of giving moral leadership. Political theory has become empirical generalizations about voting behavior rather than reflection upon the good order of political life. Most philosophers analyze the logic of the language of morals in an effort to be as value-free and scientific as the physicists. New Testament scholars cherish their academic status, and wish to become historical and literary scholars. Specialization drives the questions that moral decisions bring together into several different aspects, each of which is diligently pursued by a specialist, with no one left to view in total. Perhaps the church is being given a place—and perhaps it is too late to assume it—as the moral community, in which discourse is continuous through changing events and situations.

The Minister in the Community

The place of the minister in the deliberation has been suggested. The political analogy, suggested by Sidney Mead, might well be used here, especially if we think of political leadership in moral terms. The political leader is responsive to the consensus that exists: if this is all to which he is responsive we tend to use "political" in a pejorative sense. But he is also the shaper of the consensus, and of course, there are more and less effective and responsible ways of shaping the consensus. But if a public consensus is genuine, based not merely on adulation of a personality in politics, there is conviction and deliberation about the common good. The political leader must hear and speak; he must be informed, and inform; he must reflect and make judgments. If he is in office, he has responsibility to act; and this is one point where the analogy needs some qualification. The minister too, must act out of conviction, but obviously has a different sphere of responsibility than a government officer. But the minister can lead in the deliberations which move toward a moral consensus in the community as the participant who contributes concern and questions pertaining to the realm of the right and the good. He may not know all the data that a politician knows, or an economist knows, but he may be able to reshape the questions which bring technical data into social policy and moral action by his own moral sensibility and his practiced moral deliberation.

What I have presented is a demythologized version of a major task of the church. It has been an effort to think about what in traditional language it means to be called by God as a people, who in faithful obedience to him, seek to know and to do his will for men. It has been an effort to think about how the people who acknowledge God as Lord can responsibly serve the good of the near and distant neighbor in the preservation and cultivation of the goodness that God created for man. I am not anxious about the orthodoxy or unorthodoxy of the language: I am anxious that the religious community engage seriously and responsibly in its duties and opportunities to serve the temporal good.

Christian Conviction and Christian Action

Actions express convictions and intentions. Actions are directed by convictions and intentions. Actions assume a self-consciousness that is not characteristic of mere behavior, in which we heedlessly do what seems to come naturally to us.

The failure of certain things to occur in the human community exists because of the absence of human action pertaining to them. The absence of action in a particular realm might exist because the attention of men and their actions are immediately directed to some other realm. Or it may occur due to heedlessness, to lack of awareness that certain things ought to be done, to preoccupation with the immediate environment of life. Or actions may fail to occur because persons have no intention for certain things to occur. The failure to act is rooted in the failure to intend to be and to do certain things. The failure of intention is due sometimes to the belief that the obstacles to accomplishment are so great that it is fruitless to even think about acting. The failure of intention is also due to the lack of conviction that certain things are important, to the lack of some basic beliefs that direct intention and action toward certain issues. The failure to act is the failure to intend, and the failure to intend stems often from the failure to be convinced that things are true and right and good.

This abstract introduction contains not only the musings of a professor responding to the books in his study; it points to the nexus of relationships I have been asked to speak about, namely the way in which Christian convictions about God and man before God motivate and direct the actions of Christians in the world. It is not possible to say that because a man believes that God is made known in Jesus Christ he will necessarily picket the Red Barn Restaurant in Metropolis, North Carolina, on the afternoon of August 22 because what does not go on in that restaurant is immediately and directly contradictory to Christian belief. The fundamental religious conviction seldom has as specific implications for action as the example suggests. But it is possible to say that a person who is deeply convinced that God has revealed his care and love for all men in Jesus Christ, and who also lives in a community in which ghetto housing contributes to actual explosive human relations will be both motivated and directed by the religious conviction to certain intentions. These would be the intentions to mitigate the patent discrepancy between what God's care for men is believed to be and the dehumanizing conditions under which persons for whom God cares are forced to live. If the man is clear enough about what he most importantly believes in, is convinced enough that these beliefs are really fundamental, and is perceptive enough to see human conditions that are dissonant with the intentions that are inferred from his beliefs, he is likely to engage in action that will restore and heal human brokenness, or actions that will disrupt the unjust standing order.

Professorial abstractions have continued. Perhaps more plainly and concretely: the failure of the Christian community to be an active participant in many spheres where man's inhumanity to man are being painfully or peacefully rectified is in part a failure of conviction. This needs a bit of professorial refinement. Failure of conviction implies at least two things, both of which are important. First, Christians can have the right dogmas, the correct articulations of the basic affirmations of the church, but not have any serious conviction that they are important. Proper doctrine without a passionate relationship to the God whom the doctrine seeks to delineate hardly leads to Christian moral intentions and actions. Second, Christians can have passionate convictions about the wrong doctrines. Passionate faith that is not informed and judged by reflection about the nature of the one in whom we believe is subject to every personal and cultural perversion thinkable.

Thus I have located the task. I have hopefully outlined a case for the importance of convictions for intentions and actions, and I have indicated that the failure of the churches in the moral realms of life is due often to the lack of passion for the affirmations of the faith, or due to passions that are misplaced in what they affirm about the faith. The theological moralist cannot do much about the absence of passionate conviction: that is where the preacher and others are called to labor. He might be able to say some things about fundamental convictions of the Christian faith, which if we were passionately convinced of their validity, would both motivate and direct our intentions and our actions in the moral world.

Let us conceive of the church and its members as deputized by God to serve him in the world. The notion of deputyship has been introduced into the literature of Christian ethics by two Europeans, Dietrich Bonhoeffer and Hendrik van Oyen, and is a useful one. It suggests that the Christians have a special responsibility to God; because of their acknowledgment of him, their confession of him, they are authorized by him and obligated to him for a life of service in the world. One is not usually deputized in general; to be a deputy is to have an assigned task, it is to execute the will of the one who authorizes within the sphere of his authority. By using this notion we are not suggesting that no one but members of the Christian church is engaged in the service of God in the world. To change the metaphor, God has other masks; he works through others who do not confess his name to preserve justice and order in the world, to minister to the needs of men. Statesmen and physicians, laborers and scientists are in the service of his sovereignty even though they name no god, or call upon idols. But there is a special deputyship of the Christian community. It is, in effect, partially a response to God's goodness and God's judgment which we know in human life and in our faith. It is partially the response of gratitude and gladness, the service that is given in the joy of being the unmerited recipients of a goodness we have not earned.

Our deputyship is also a willful commitment on the part of the church. We respond to God's call, and register our consent to being under obligation to his will and his way. Some of our forefathers in faith talked about this in terms of covenant: For what God has done for man, men in turn agree to do certain things for God.

I am stressing the importance of a commitment to serve God as his deputies because we live in a time when the idea of obligations and binding covenants is not popular among many Christians. There are many who would like to think that somehow God's life and love flow through the lives and loves of men without regard to a conscious reflection about what is in accord with God's work and ways. Faith and the authentic expression of one's being sometimes authorize activities without critical reflection about the one whom men are called to serve.

Whose deputies are we in the church? God's, presumably. The answer is clear enough. But the content we believe to be present in our reference to God is exceedingly important in understanding the nature and purpose of our deputyship. I can hardly stress this enough. What we believe about God and his purposes delineates the scope of our responsibilities as his deputies. This can be illustrated rather easily.

If a Christian group believes that God's intentions are almost exclusively to redeem men from their private lives of sins, its activities will be largely confined to the seeking to convince men of their sin, and bringing them to an acknowledgment that Christ died for their sins. What is left out is what I wish to note. There is no serious inclusion of the conviction that the God who acts to save men from sin is also the God who acts creatively to bring life into the world, and who acts to preserve and order the existence of the human community. The majestic scope of the sovereignty of God is whittled down to a particular, though of course important aspect of his work. If the God in whom I believe is only the God who saves individuals from sin, my agency under him is limited to bringing others to the recognition that they need their sins forgiven too.

If a Christian group believes that God's concerns for man are charitable, in the most popular sense of that word, its activities will be charitable in the same sense. God seeks to overcome suffering among his children, so his deputies found hospitals and orphanages as agents of God's will. There is no serious inclusion of the belief that God is concerned not only with the relief of human suffering, but with the sources and causes of human suffering. Such religious convictions do not motivate and direct action in the impersonal spheres of state and economic order, and in the founding of educational institutions, but in the establishment of the institutions of public charity.

If a Christian group believes God is to be depicted in terms of an infinite reality of acceptance of the foibles of men, as a fountain of therapy, its activities will center on distributing the benefits of God's acceptability and therapy to emotionally distraught souls. If a group thinks of God as lord of a realm of spirituality, and if it has successfully done what the biblical writers could not do, namely separate spirituality from embodiment in flesh, its ministry will be directed (falsely) to some notion of spirituality that also never enters the flesh and blood of personal and social existence.

Enough for illustrations. What men believe about God delineates the contours of their responsibilities as his deputies. This is why Christian ethics has a very heavy stake in how the church understands God and his purposes and activities. It is not a matter of merely speculative interest; it is a matter of practical interest.

The Bible gives fairly ample testimony to the experience of both the old and the new Israel that God is ill-conceived if he is not seen to be sovereign Lord over all things. If one sparrow can fall without God's concern, we have something less than God. If one event in history can occur without his involvement (hard as it is to see it, not to mention foresee it), we have conveniently reduced God to man's comfortable dimensions. There is no doubt that the affirmation of God's rule brings with it a host of theological problems, and there is no doubt that the full realization of God's sovereign good rule is part of Christian hope more than present Christian experience. But the point I wish to make does not rest here; it rests in the affirmation that the God who calls us to deputyship is the lord over all things. The implication for deputyship is by now clear. To be the deputy of the sovereign God is to have responsibility for all things; it is not to leave out certain spheres of life as being outside the realm of Christian moral responsibility. Obviously we cannot attend to everything everywhere; we are limited as deputies to our bodies, our talents, our time and place. But we cannot arbitrarily decide that something is outside of the scope of Christian moral responsibility.

One particular emphasis needs to be made when we are concerned with the action of the church in society; God is lord not just of persons, but of the relationships and institutions in and through which persons exist. His rule and his work to be sure are addressed to my personal existence, and to those of each man. But the pattern of his sovereign work in the world extends beyond individual entities and their needs and requirements; he is lord of human life together, of the concentrations of power in institutions and particular offices that men fill in them, of not just a father and a son, but of the relationship between a father and a son. This is why it is quite proper in the church's prayers of intercessions to pray not just for a congressman but for Congress, not just for Richard Nixon, but for the President of the United States, not just for U Thant, but for the United Nations. Excessive concentration on God's will and way for persons too often loses sight of God's will and way for the impersonal, and shrinks the scope of God's sovereignty and in turn the scope of human Christian responsibility.

We are deputies of the sovereign God. But is this God only a grand principle of order and power that finally puts unity into the many persons and things that occur? Or can we say more about him? Joseph Sittler reminds us that for the biblical people "God is what God manifestly does." What kinds of things did the biblical people perceive God to be doing? What theologians answer in abstract words the biblical people narrated in concrete descriptive terms, and Jesus clarified in parables. What does God do? He leads a whole people out of social and spiritual bondage in the land of Egypt, even when many of them longed for the security of their slavery, and even when their former masters pursued them with a sense of civil order and propriety. What does God do? He distills his ordering work into a series of commandments that indicate what life in relation to God and other men is meant to be. He intervenes in the relations between the nations so that peoples are made to suffer for their injustice and unrighteousness. He tenderly receives his unfaithful, harlotrous children in his mercy. He scornfully and awesomely refuses sometimes to speak the word of comfort that men badly need and cherish. He brings order into chaos, and does not hesitate to introduce disorder into false and unjust order. He gives and takes life. His rule is like a mustard seed, or it is a kind of indiscriminating care that is not bound to pay a person according to the standards of human measurement. On some occasions he appears to be the restrainer of evil, on others he permits men to suffer from the evil of others. The whole range of nature, historical, and personal experience is interpreted from time to time with reference to God's sovereign rule. God makes his Son to suffer and to die, without promise of an earthly reward and kingdom. And yet, Paul tells the Corinthians that all things are theirs, for they are Christ's and Christ is God's.

The rehearsal could go on and on, but for Bible-reading Presbyterians it is not necessary to extend it. From the rehearsal different theologians have made different generalized affirmations and different emphases among their affirmations about God. And the choices they make again affect the ways in which they delineate the responsibilities of deputyship. Again some illustrations will make the point.

Paul Lehmann, in *Ethics in a Christian Context,* affirms the freedom of God. God does surprising things, and only at his peril does man try to set up the rules that he infers from what he believes God to have done in the past. In his freedom God is doing humanizing work. He is seeking to resist those things that dehumanize man, and enhancing those things that enable man to be human. This much Lehmann will say. What then is the Christian deputyship? It is to be immediately sensitive to what God in his freedom is doing to make life human. Christians are to discern what God is doing for the humanity of men, and to make their actions coincide with this. Stated in this way, which is not my own preference as a way to state the case, our deputyship is given scope and direction. We ought to be involved wherever life is suffering from dehumanization. If it is the terrifying domination of a mother over her daughter, the church has a moral pastoral responsibility. If a man is becoming animalized as a result of alcoholism, there is a place for our agency. If the customary forms of social relations, and the legal bulwarks given to them prohibit some human beings from having the liberties and opportunities granted to other human beings, the church is called to activity. Why? Because God has revealed himself to be one who is for man, who seeks the humanization of man in Christ Jesus.

Or, in Reinhold Niebuhr's theology, God is delineated in terms of perfect love, agape. This love, in Niebuhr's emphasis, is the self-sacrificial love made painfully visible on the cross. This love of God is at once the empowering of the Christian community and its unachievable norm. What do a people who acknowledge God then do? They act through and in the light of this love in all their relationships, but particularly in those which most patently deny the reality of this love. Thus wherever men are related to men, there needs to be an approximation of this love—in the personal bonds of family, but also in the impersonal ordering of life through civil law and through the state. Love is the law of life—all of life. The scope is again universal; the direction of action is given by the basic conviction that God is love—indiscriminating, self-sacrificial love.

For traditional Lutheran theology God works through the gospel and through the law. Through the gospel he acts to redeem men from sin, and makes them a gift of his righteousness. They are to act in relation to the neighbor in faith, through love, in a sense recapitulating for the neighbor's need the love that God gave for their deepest need. Through the law God acts not only to convict men of sin, but also to preserve order in a world in which chaos always threatens. So what is the Christian deputyship? It is finally in both realms—to be motivated to do the deeds of love in the realm of the personal with an indiscrimination and graciousness that reenacts God's love. It is to serve in the place in the world to which God has called a man, doing the duties that make for justice and order as a servant of God.

Theologians generalize from the rehearsal of the deeds of God, and order their preferences according to fundamental convictions of their own. This is not the place to argue about those convictions in detail. It is the place to stress once again that what Christians believe about God, how they chose to speak about the one in whom they trust, provides the ground for their moral intentions and actions in their deputyship in the world. In one way or another, with one stress or another, the church has said that God is sovereign, and that he works creatively in nature and history and human activity, that he preserves the world that he has created, that he rules and judges it, and that he seeks ever to redeem it from its unfaithfulness and destruction. So great is the authorization of the Christian community, and so awesome is the responsibility of its deputyship: to be the agents of the sovereign God, seeking to fulfill his purposes.

But Christian conviction is not the only ingredient in Christian action. The deputy is genuinely an agent, in that he has the freedom to act under his authorization as his situation and time demand. The deputized Christian community lives between the authorizing sovereign God and the world in which his sovereign purposes are to be effected. Indeed, it lives in that world, is a part of that world. Its responsibility to God is for the world in which it lives. Thus the church has to be perceptive and morally sensitive to what is going on in family life and international relations, the civil rights struggle and the effects of an era of normlessness in which adolescents now come to maturity. The church needs to use the information and the categories of analysis that best enable it to understand what is occurring in human lives, and in the civil and social orders.

The moral intentions of the Christian community are not simply deduced from some general statements about the nature of God's rule. They are shaped both with reference to historical biblical convictions and with reference to the acutely particularized events and persons in history's field of activity. We know this to be the case really, even if we sometimes forget this fact. We obey the commandment "Thou shalt not kill" in a literal way under normal circumstances, but circumstances are not always normal. There are the borderline occasions in war and self-defense, sometimes in medical care and in the pursuit of justice that lead conscientious Christians to discern conscientiously that it is proper to take life under unusual circumstances. I wish to affirm that the kind of thinking we are forced to do in relating Christian conviction to intentions and actions in borderline cases we also ought to be doing in situations that do not strike us as to be unusual or inflammatory.

It is in this open field between identifiable Christian conviction on one side and participation in occasions and events on the other side that the moral discourse of the churches takes place. "Open field" suggests a spatial imagery; such is only partially accurate. The openness is also in present time; what Christians are doing and are not doing this day affects to some extent the course of personal lives and social events in the days that are to come. Indeed, the location of the openness is in us as human beings, who are gifted with the ability to initiate and condition events by our self-conscious intention and action. The churches are not necessarily involved in Christian action of a morally significant sort if they are only getting their Christian convictions in order. Moral intentions are shaped by the process of discourse and reflection as the churches ask, "What are we to be doing here?" in the light of faith in God, whose work is understood in terms of divine sovereignty. The questions of moral activity, to be sure, must be given focus, and usually, like fire fighters, we attend to the most inflammatory situations as they emerge without our willful participation in their emergence.

Some measure of passion about our faith in God, informed by stated conviction about the nature and activity of God, should help to make us morally sensitive to the moral needs of men and society. Obviously other factors are involved in the presence or absence of a high degree of moral sensitivity in addition to religious convictions: some persons seem to be psychologically crippled and thus morally rusty; all of us continue to be turned inward upon ourselves as the center of truth and concern and thus readily find many reasons for moral apathy on egocentric grounds. This is true for churches as well as persons. Institutional concerns become more central than the intentions that are derived from asking what deputyship to the sovereign God implies for worldly life. Passion about God, passionate faith in God, requires the process of theological and moral reflection if our capacities for moral discernment are to be sensitive to the needs of man. Christian conviction, impassioned by faith in the one about whom we are convinced, should be both a motivating and sensitizing force in the moral life of the churches. Thus Christian conviction is not only a matter of the life of the mind, and its function in Christian action is not circumscribed by the uses of human reason to derive moral imperatives that are consistent with theological indicatives.

For a morally self-conscious Christian community, however, this use of moral reflection is also a part of deputyship. The relation between conviction and action, while not exhausted by our rational capacity to shape intentions that are consonant with convictions, is one that requires as lively and careful attention as the intellectual life of the churches can give it. There is no substitute for the vocation to reflect clearly on what Christians ought to be doing in the world. There is no substitute for this reflection whether at the assembly level, the synodical level, or the level of the congregation. The rewards might be meager; indeed they might be hostility rather than public favor. But serious commitment to God requires serious reflection about what actions and intentions express God's will and way in highly concrete places and times and for specific persons.

This task too is part of Christian conviction; it is part of the theological foundations of Christian action, even though it is carried out in ethical language rather than precisely theological language. The church is not an extension of an electronic network whose control board is operated by God, and whose activities are governed solely by those impulses. God has always called his people to a relationship of responsibility to him, to an agency in which the agent has the capacity and the obligation to decide and to act under authorization, but nevertheless to decide and to act. We exist in relation to God and man as a community and as persons able to make mistakes, to pervert intentions and actions by unfaithfulness to God and to man, to risk consequences of our initiation of influence and direction into the course of events. What Christian ethical reflection can do is a modest task, namely aid in seeking to make the intentions and actions of the church and of Christians consonant with the convictions about God and the needs of humanity.

Christian action expresses Christian conviction, and intentions formed in relation to that body of conviction. The actions of the conscientious Christian are directed in part by his convictions about God, in whom he believes, and by intentions inferred from those convictions, but also related to the particular occasions of his moral responsibility. Our convictions are that God, made known through his deeds in Israel's perception of them, and in the face of Jesus Christ as the apostles have depicted it to us, is the sovereign Lord of all things. To be deputized by him is to be particularly responsible to him for the things over which he is Lord. No person, no event can be arbitrarily left out of our concern. And certainly the particular events and persons in our particular spheres of life give location to our deputyship. To fulfill this is to think carefully about God's will and way, to be perceptive with reference to our world, to be sensitized and directed by our faith and conviction, and to shape our intentions and actions with clarity. It is also to acknowledge that we are *only* deputies, and subject to the limitations and perversions of agency. God remains sovereign, and we live in hope as well as in solemn moral obligation.

The
Voluntary Church:
A Moral Appraisal

Amerian Protestantism is made up of "voluntary churches."
This is true in several senses. The freedom to be religious in the
manner of a man's own choice and the freedom to be nonreligious
are guaranteed by the basic law of our land. Thus, from a legal
point of view all religious groups are noncompulsory; there is no
legal means for compelling church affiliation. Church membership is by consent. Even those churches with a "high" doctrine
of infant baptism are in effect voluntary churches. Membership is
not complete upon baptism; it must be confirmed in more mature years. In some instances, baptism and confirmation are not
sufficient for church membership; decision and commitment after
conversion are required. American Protestantism is radically "con-
gregationalized." Many churches are of a congregational tradition in polity, and others have been democratized so that the
voice of the laity bears more weight than is characteristic in many
European Evangelical churches. The congregationalizing is not
only political: Protestantism and even Catholicism in America
seek to develop a common life among the members of a congregation, either as a whole or through various societies and groups.
Finally, American Christianity is voluntary in the sense that it
stresses activity and action, an exertion of the will for moral or
evangelical purposes.

The contemporary American voluntary churches are rather
different from the Puritan conception of the gathered church.

The kind of clarity in definition of basis of membership, social control, and common discipline that informed the earlier gathered-church notion exists in only a few sects. The Puritan gathered church had three tests for membership: the experience of regenerating grace, right belief, and upright conduct. With a certainty unknown to their descendants, the Puritans believed that certain human experiences were sure and certain signs of the efficacious work of Divine Grace, that the proper definition of God could be captured in written documents, and that a man's behavior would reveal the quality of his religious faith. Since the seventeenth century, there has been an almost irresistible development of the gathered church into its compromised forms. The "gathered church" has become the "voluntary church." The decisive criterion is now the will to belong. The theological and experiential marks of authority on which the in-group was defined from the out-group have lost their power. The zest for purity in the churches has given way to an acceptance of the impossibility of its achievement, and consequently to a more or less open membership. Now, instead of being gathered out of the body of strangers into the family of saints, the strangers volunteer to join the community of those like themselves, who find something meaningful in religious life for themselves, their children, or their neighborhood. Men admire the saints among them, and perhaps wish to join their small number. If they fail, however, there is no serious disruption of church life.

The Bases of Belonging

As a result of the acceptance of the "will to belong" as the functioning basis for church membership, the principles that delineate the in-group from the out-group have shifted. The loose way in which the word parish is used illustrates the contemporary confusion. At one time a parish was a geographical mark of belonging, as it still is in parts of Europe. Now the word is used to refer to the people who belong to a congregation, together with their families and friends. At an earlier time it made sense to refer to a congregation gathered out of a parish; now the words "parish" and "congregation" are often used interchangeably. (In the national churches of Northern Europe "parish" and "congregation" are coextensive for reasons other than the misuse of the word parish. The "folk-church" idea is expressed in the almost universal baptism and confirmation of children, and thus almost everyone residing in the geographical territory of the parish is a member of the "congregation.") The geographical mark of parish is not very important in the voluntary church, for the place of residence is not decisive in determining the particular congregation that a family joins. The will to belong is more significant than place of residence for a family's "parish" identification. The threefold test of membership in the gathered church is thoroughly compromised, if not completely lost, and thus the religious in-group exercises relatively little theological and moral discrimination about the persons who choose to join it. The net effect is that various social and social-psychological factors become the operating principles in the determination of church membership. The voluntary church in a secularized society is at the mercy of powerful social forces in the determination of its social boundaries.

Much evidence supports this suggestion. It is common for people to join a church in their "neighborhood." But neighborhoods no longer coincide with the political boundaries of a town, or with the ancient boundaries of a Catholic parish. In metropolitan areas the neighborhood is defined by characteristics of housing, which in a large measure reflect the level of family income. This, in turn, is governed by the achievement of the employed members of the family, often the father alone. His achievement is a product of his education, the marketability of his personality and talent, and his drive toward success. In short, the neighborhood is generally defined by the combination of factors that are used to indicate a family's position in the social stratification of the society, its social class. Thus it is common for the members of churches in a particular neighborhood to be a relatively homogeneous group.

In nonmetropolitan areas the neighborhood cannot always be defined by housing without strained efforts of gerrymandering. But this does not in itself prevent a social selectivity in church membership. With the variety of American denominations, it is usual for the prospective church member to choose among several

options. He might find the church in which the liturgy is most
meaningful (which may mean whose decorum is congenial to his
socially defined tastes), or the church that provides the kind of
preaching he likes (which may mean that which least threatens
his personal and social defenses), or the church whose members
are more like himself than the members of the other available
churches are. The evidence from American community studies
which indicates the relative social prestige of various congregations and denominations in villages and towns is by now part of the
sociological commonplace. It suggests a functional relationship
between membership in a particular church and one's present or
hoped-for social status. Thus the congregation is at the mercy of
the image of cultural and social achievement and aspiration that
it represents.

Social class, however, is not the only factor at work. Since the
generations of vast immigration, the national loyalties of people
have often determined their church membership. Even the Roman Catholic Church, which has had more success than any other
group in transplanting the geographical parish principle to a
voluntaristic culture and society, bowed to the pressure for national churches. St. Casimir's, St. Stanislaus', and St. Anthony's
parishes are still likely to represent the religious centers of the
Lithuanian, Polish, and Italian populations of a middle-sized
American city. Among Protestants the Lutheran denominations
have been the obvious example of ethnic religious loyalties.
Lutherans in one city might be divided among the Norwegians,
the Swedes, the Finns, and the Germans. Only now, after a century and more of life on this continent, are most of these Lutheran groups finding a basis of unity that transcends national
heritage. (The basis found may be more a generalized American-
ization of third and fourth generations than a common loyalty to
the objective teachings and liturgies of Lutherdom.) Presbyte-
rianism and the Disciples of Christ have represented "American"
churches in the eyes of Protestant immigrants, i.e., churches of the
Anglo-Saxon population.

More visible than social class or nationality groupings is the
racially selective character of American church life. The racial
loyalty and identification of the white community becomes the

basis for a voluntary principle of exclusion. The Negro community has, in the main, no option other than to organize religious life on a racial basis. Historically, the picture is more complex, for the church has been the institution in which characteristic expressions of both religious and cultural life have been made. The social situation of the Negro in America, now undergoing rapid change, has been the milieu for a combination of religious and racial identity. The enforced segregation of churches based upon the racial voluntarism of the white population, and the cultural situation of the Negro population that has had its own religious expressions, are both social factors at the base of church life. In contrast to this, a Christian community gathered around the more objective centers of its life—Jesus Christ, the Bible, a creed, or a historic liturgy—would have no place for a racial basis of the right or the will to belong.

The Pervasiveness of Voluntarism

Denominational and interdenominational patterns of life, like local congregations, also testify to the voluntary order of participation and organization.

The same socially selective principles that work in local congregations are effective at the denominational level. Tendencies toward domination by a single class in various denominations are significant enough to make possible a rank order of American Protestantism on the basis of social status. In the main the denominations are racially segregated, with at best hardly more than token integration in any of the major ones. Nationality background, while declining in significance, is still the basis of differentiation for a number of denominations.

The patterns of ecclesiastical organization are generally democratic, with variations in form; for examples, the popular democracy of the Disciples of Christ, and the representational democracy of the Presbyterians. The affairs of the denominations are carried on in the light of the necessity for the consent and support of the laity. Interest groups among the lay membership have significant influence in setting limits to ecclesiastical policy when their points of view are threatened. This has been seen in recent decades among the major Protestant churches in the sphere of social action. The dependence upon voluntary financial support is the agency through which lay dissent can be most powerfully registered.

Interdenominational activity in local Councils of Churches, or at state and national levels, is subject to most of the same mechanisms of government and consent that one sees in denominations. Their effectiveness in part depends upon the broadest possible support for the organization, which in turn requires highly sensitive antennae to register the presence or absence of "grassroots" support. Like denominations, they are subject to the reluctance of the laity to grant independence of authority to elected and appointed church officials to speak for the church, particularly on moral issues.

Social Ethics and the Voluntary Church

The voluntary character of American church life affects the concern for social ethics at three points. First, there are detriments to, and possibilities for, effective social education and action given by the voluntary social character of Protestantism, especially by its tendency toward single-class congregations. Protestantism's participation in American social stratification and cultural values is two-sided: there are sociologically inevitable restrictions on the freedom of the church to speak and to act; and there are sociological possibilities for a lay church with access to some centers of social action in the society.

The voluntary sociological pattern raises the issue of authority in the churches. In the voluntary church, the question of authority takes particular form, namely, who speaks and acts for the churches? Theological principles and sociological structures are not harmonious with each other on this question. The voluntary church is Christ's church; but the "will to belong" does not give a sufficient basis to permit a congregational majority to speak for Christ. A covetous glance at the structure of Roman Catholicism with its views of hierarchy and priesthood cannot be satisfied. Institutional authority of a Catholic sort is both unrealistic on sociological grounds and unacceptable on theological grounds for Protestantism in America. The issue of authority is common to all democratically oriented voluntary associations, namely, the relation of popular support to effective leadership. But it takes unique form in the churches: the church acknowledges and knows a higher authority—God; but the voluntary churches are not sure who speaks and acts for him.

Thus the third point becomes clearer. What theological and socio-theological principles help us to understand what voluntary Protestantism in America can be? What can the great Christian affirmations of the work of the Holy Spirit or the presence of Christ mean in the voluntaristic church? Is the voluntary church theologically and morally viable? The remainder of this essay deals with these three issues.

Moral Hindrances and Possibilities at the Social Level

The social determination of the churches has wide implications for their nature as moral communities. Indeed, if a "moral" community indicates one with distinctive values that are propagated and acted upon within the group, there is evidence to doubt the existence of the church as a unique body. The consensus of values is likely to express the dominant cultural orientation of the church. At least the evidence is highly mixed; on empirical grounds, as many sociological and psychological studies have indicated, grave doubts are raised about the power of distinctively Christian ethics to shape the attitudes and outlooks, as well as the actions, of people. Some of the social factors involved require further delineation.

What factors make for social homogeneity in churches? The reasons why people belong to particular churches appear to be accidental in relation to any differentiating norms that mark the church off from other groups, or mark one Protestant congregation off from another. The urban church ecologists have shown how difficult it is to maintain a socially heterogeneous congregation in a geographical area that tends to be single-class in residential constituency. The wider movements of population, often called the "invasion-succession" patterns, tend to determine the characteristics of members of churches, as well as other institutions in a neighborhood. Ideological as well as racial and economic factors are involved. That is, persons gather together around certain values that are held in common, or certain symbols of status toward which they aspire. Urbanism, to quote the title of a deservedly famous essay of Louis Wirth, is "a way of life." So, one might add, are suburbanism, and the romance of the small town. The ways of life that bring people together in given areas, or form the bonds of unity among them, are brought into church life as well. Sometimes the identification with the status symbols of a group seems to require the "transfer" of church membership to another congregation if not another denomination.

Residential patterns and common ways of life are not alone in supporting social homogeneity in churches. The long leadership of a particular pastor may build up a particular "clientele" of those who find his preaching or pastoral work congenial. A local congregation might well become accepted in local tradition as one that appeals to a particular social or intellectual group by virtue of its leadership and program. In a relatively stable community, such a tradition can survive for a long time.

The tendency toward social homogeneity in American congregations presents the great temptation to equate the socially acceptable patterns of life, the approved ways of thinking and acting, with the truth of the gospel itself. An antidote to this temptation would be to create or preserve social heterogeneity within the churches. This would provide diversity of thought and opinion, and thus would temper the tendency to confuse socially conditioned ways of work, thought, and life with Christian ways. If multi-group churches are to be possible, certain social factors usually must be at work.

What factors make for social heterogeneity in churches? One might assume that the relatively stable small community would make possible social diversity in churches. Presumably, here the ethos of democracy exists at the grass roots, and status lines are of no significance. The empirical evidence from small community studies, however, points in the other direction. In James West, *Plainville, U.S.A.*, a study of a small Missouri town, and in Vidich and Bensman, *Small Town in Mass Society*, a more recent study of a New York State community, ample evidence is given to indicate a sharp differentiation along locally defined status lines even in the small town.

It is clear that the social stratification affects the life of the churches. The unfortunate fact of rabid competition between denominations and sects in America's small towns is well known. Four or five congregations struggling for survival in towns of five hundred people is not uncommon across the land. The availability of options for church membership lends itself to choosing the congregation that is most socially congenial, even in hamlets. And in both of the studies mentioned, there is also evidence of a "de-classed" population, which exists outside of the range of any of the sects. In parts of rural New England, where the religious culture is somewhat more stable (i.e., where there is clearer domination of two or three Protestant denominations), there is evidence of greater social heterogeneity in congregations, but it does not alter the general picture. The small church in the small town is seldom socially inclusive in membership.

A factor that would make for heterogeneity is a nonclass center of loyalty that is stronger than class identification. Perhaps the most common in parts of the United States is the ethnic loyalty. Descendants of the immigrants from a particular nation may have a residual (and sometimes more vital) identification with their ethnic group through the church; for example, the Norwegians of a small Minnesota town. Class inclusiveness has been minimized, however, by sizable migrations out of ethnic churches by the socially mobile members.

Loyalty to a liturgical or creedal tradition might be the most effective religious-social phenomenon to overcome class determination. In the case of many Lutheran congregations, one has the combination of creedal, liturgical, and ethnic components. In the case of the Protestant Episcopal Church, one sees the importance of a more objective and uniform liturgical pattern. In principle, the existence of more objective points of reference for ecclesiastical life should make possible a more inclusive church on the social level. Whether or not this is the case depends in part upon the absence of several congregations within the same creedal or liturgical tradition, each representing a particular class. Where, for example, several Protestant Episcopal churches are available in a middle-sized or large American city, they are often socially stratified within the denomination. The population in the neighborhood is one factor that makes this so; the ease with which persons can travel to a congenial congregation is another. In order for creed and liturgy to function as points transcending class identification, a small and relatively stable population seems to be necessary.

Special efforts to maintain diversity occur in most American denominations. Often the most dramatic examples of multi-class or multiracial churches, however, are maintained only during a transitional period in the life of a neighborhood. This is especially true in the large cities. A congregation can maintain a multiracial constituency during the period in which the residential pattern of its neighborhood is multiracial. When the white community moves away en masse, as it usually does, the valiant efforts of pastors and laity to form a congregation gathered without reference to race or class often fade away. Our cities are studded with church buildings that once housed white middle or upper-middle class congregations which declined as this group moved toward the periphery of the area, then became interracial as Negroes or other groups "invaded" the area, and after a decade in this laudable inclusive pattern have tended to become almost exclusively Negro congregations.

Another pattern is the deliberate establishment of new congregations on interracial or multi-class lines. Aside from a certain theological artificiality in this procedure, other difficulties are presented. The characteristics of the ministry, reinforced by its pattern of training, often make such congregations acceptable only to persons of certain educational or social achievements. One may simply substitute, for example, multiracial single-class churches for single-racial single-class churches. Dominantly Negro pentecostal movements that seek to be inclusive are limited in their attraction to white persons not only because of racial prejudice, but also because the patterns of church life are alien to the social and intellectual expectations of educated white persons. The same selectivity might operate on other levels; emancipated, educated, socially free whites and Negroes can belong together in a multiracial congregation, but a social principle of selectivity is probably still at work.

The social and cultural conditions that create and sustain in-

clusive churches seldom occur in American society. The forces
that make for status differentiation along economic, racial, and
educational lines in the society as a whole are difficult to overcome within the life of the churches. While heterogeneity in congregations would provide a social basis for overcoming the temptation to confuse socially conditioned patterns of life with those
that are divinely ordained and approved, the achievement is itself dependent upon the very human stuff of society and church.

Voluntary churches cannot expect the optimum conditions under which to achieve the purposes and mission of a people called
to be obedient to Christ any more than ambitious intellectuals
can free themselves from the fatigue that is part of their bodily
existence. The human social conditions under which the church
exists is part of the stuff of its life. The problems and possibilities
for a Christian moral community under the given social conditions can be assessed more precisely.

Problems of a Socially Heterogeneous Church

The socially inclusive congregation may have difficulties in
maintaining interaction and communication between persons representing various socially defined groups. The distinctions between the college-educated and those without higher learning,
the bankers and the welders, the farmers and the urbane sophis-
ticates, the adolescents from economically affluent families and
those from economically marginal families, all make the processes
of forming a moral community difficult. The points of social and
cultural differentiation are not dropped upon entering the portals
of the House of God. The acknowledgment of a universal center
of loyalty and common life does not in itself create a common
vocabulary, a common definition of human needs, a common outlook on the purpose and mission of the church, or a common
basis of interpersonal relationships.

One often finds as a result that clear social differentiations
take place *within* a congregation. For example, in the recruit-
ment of lay leadership for the church, there is a tendency to select
persons who have achieved positions of leadership in voluntary
associations or vocations outside of the church. The reasons for
this are complex. In part the experience and talent that make a

person conspicuous in the secular world are often precisely those needed for effective organization in a church. Competence in teaching, in financial matters, in public address and parliamentary procedure, and in exerting influence to gain support for various activities all have utility in the church as well as outside. From a critical point of view, one notes that it is not always easy for talented laymen to revise their ways of work in the light of the theologically defined purposes that govern the life of the church. The norms by which effectiveness are judged in church life are not necessarily the same as those used in other organizations. Thus, a redirection, if not a transformation, of the ways of work of the talented might be hoped for but is not always forthcoming.

The selection of leadership, however, is not always made on the grounds of the utility of talents. It is sometimes motivated by the prestige that the high secular status of the laymen might bring to the church. The capturing and borrowing of prestige often takes place apart from any religious-social rationality that might be involved. There is evidence of this in various phases of congregational life. Some ministers take obvious delight when they can claim a socially prominent person to be a leader in their church. Indeed, occasionally one finds a minister who identifies himself as the pastor of "Mr. Corporation President's Church." Another evidence of prestige-borrowing is in the financial campaigns of the churches. This particular gimmick, for example, was an important device in the high-powered, professionally run fund-raising campaigns of the past decade in American church life. The commitment of the high-status man has the effect of initiating a falling row of dominoes for all who seek some social identification with him.

Another instance of social differentiation within inclusive congregations takes place in various organized groups within the church. Age-groupings, for example, have commonly divided various women's groups from each other. The level of interest intended in a particular program can become socially selective and inadvertently call attention to sharp diversities. This can be seen in the development of fairly high-level study programs for adults. The nature of the material to be studied acts as a factor of social differentiation. Furthermore, voluntary groups in churches are often divided by the formation of cliques within them. Men's and women's groups are sometimes divided by factors of social congeniality, and by the absorption into church life of friendship groups primarily directed by life in the residential community. The evidence of the adolescent cliques, drawn often along lines of locally defined status, is apparent to most youth workers. The evidence analyzed by August Hollingshead, for example, in *Elmtown's Youth*, presents hypotheses for the activities of young people in churches that are almost immediately confirmed on the basis of both unrefined and more disciplined impressions.

Leadership is difficult in a socially diverse congregation. In most Protestant denominations, promotional and educational material is clearly directed, though probably unintentionally so, to a broad middle class. Stewardship leaflets, church school material, denomination journals, official reports of denominational agencies, and other published literature reflect the cultural and social orientations dominant among the writers and the sponsors. Evidence indicates that for Protestantism as a whole a middle-class target is probably accurate, but it is not always easy for Negroes and Puerto Ricans of the inner city to identify themselves with the literature, nor is it certain that techniques devised in New York to be effective among Protestant suburbanites will work in marginal churches on the plains of North Dakota, in spite of the nationalization of taste and values.

Ministerial leadership is confronted with special problems by social inclusiveness. If not by social origin, then by education and training, a social distance is created between the minister and those groups in his church who are marginal to his own educational, social, and cultural dispositions. Effective communication with those who do not share the minister's own cultural milieu is difficult. There is no evidence that the minister, any more than the layman, is necessarily emancipated from his own social biases by virtue of his religious faith or his theological education. His professional and social aspirations, as well as those of his family, are likely to orient his patterns of life and ways of work in a direction more toward one group than another in the congregation.

The difficulties enumerated indicate that it is by no means a simple step from social diversity to the development of a religious and moral community in which a consensus comes into being. Yet social diversity offers clear possibilities toward this end that do not exist in more homogeneous religious groups.

Possibilities of a Socially Heterogeneous Church

Social diversity makes more visible the normative and essential inclusiveness of the religious and moral community. Where there are rather obvious marks of differentiation on a very human level, one is likely to become aware that the center of life in this group is in part removed from the human sameness. The existence of people representing different races, economic states of life, educational achievement, and political points of view in one congregation calls more vivid attention to the love, the forgiveness, the life, and the meanings that the church represents on a universal plane. The actual human materials that make up the complexes of races and cultures existing in the worldwide church have to some extent a microcosmic reflection in a heterogeneous local congregation. Thus the drive toward inclusiveness that is present at the heart of the Christian gospel can be manifest, not to demonstrate a kind of tolerance, nor to show that persons of different life-orientations can live together in a given voluntary association, but to testify to the unity that is in Jesus Christ. The acceptance of diversity is then the religious and social implication of the acknowledgment of a common Lord of life.

The richness of the inclusive church is manifest in other ways. The physical presence of heterogeneity makes it more difficult for a congregation to confuse a particular social mode of life with the religiously acceptable and divinely ordained one. For example, if believers in the welfare state who have a clear Christian devotion and articulate Christian convictions are in conversation with those who believe in the sanctity of the free market, the potential idolatry of either pattern might be limited. But this function of a negative check against idolatry can be turned into something more fruitful in the moral community.

Diversity in a congregation ought to make possible the social and intellectual interaction out of which two important things can occur. First, and most likely, persons with different political and social orientations can become better informed about the bases of judgment of those whom they oppose. Their own thinking might come not only to include a new measure of tolerance for other points of view, but also be modified. The congregation, in meeting, might become a place in which, under the common center of faith, the points of view of persons are developed. The common point of community life, the Christian gospel, might be brought to bear upon the judgments and opinions of various persons. They could possibly see new facets or dimensions in the realm of social and political judgments: dimensions of morality, and finally of faith.

Second, and more difficult, would be the development of some significant moral consensus within the congregation. Moral consensus brought into being under the conditions of social and cultural diversity could not be simply the projection of the ideology of a particular interest group on the screen of divine approval. Rather, it would represent the processes of growth toward community based on a common faith and loyalty shared by different groups. In a voluntary church in which lay participation is more than an expression of the will to belong, there might be the study and conversation that could meaningfully lead to the formation of some common expression of opinion. The religious conditions presumably are present in essence, if not in actuality. These, in contemporary parlance, are the members' acceptance of each other as persons, and not as the manifestations of partial interests or partial functions. Such acceptance would be the social counterpart to the common experience of standing under God's judgment, receiving God's forgiveness, and sharing together in the new life in Christ. Under these religious conditions, one might expect candid and informed exchange of opinion and ideas about responsibility in the world. The imperative element is also present, for common loyalty to Jesus Christ requires that thinking and judgment be brought under the discipline of seeking a way of life and action commensurate with the norms of this community.

The realization of the possibilities latent in the socially inclusive church requires a voluntarism of a different sort than that implied in the will to belong. It depends upon a genuine exercise of the will on the part of the leadership of the church, and on the part of the persons who share more passively in its life. Persons, and hopefully congregations together, would have to exercise the capacity to make decisions under reflection and discussion. Such an achievement in church life is not to be expected in any mass movement, but perhaps will be done in those centers where laity and clergy accept in grace the determination of the will to shape personal and corporate life in the image of God's work and will.

Problems and Possibilities of a Socially Homogeneous Church

In a sense that pricks the conscience of reflective Christians, most congregations are already moral communities. A latent if not explicit consensus already exists on the major things to be desired in life, the major purposes to be achieved in history, and the principles by which judgments are made. The dissatisfaction comes with the impression that the moral consensus reflects social homogeneity, rather than a community that wills to become a center of life in Jesus Christ. Some aspects of this problematic character have been suggested. A rehearsal of these, however, ought not to keep us from accepting such homogeneity as a place of opportunity for moral witness and action. Some aspects of this opportunity can also be specified.

The problems of a socially determined moral consensus in churches have been most noted in suburbia, but they are by no means there exclusively. The same mistaken identification of the divinely approved order with the social style of life that occurs in Park Forest, Illinois, occurs also in Lanyon, Iowa. The actual patterns that are given community approval differ, but principle is the same. This mistake is made in part because of the absence among church members of diversity in experience and perspectives. The parochialism, or provincialism, leads to a limited view of the world; the absence of diverse groups limits the contact with other subcultures. The blissful freedom from conflict, or presence of harmony that men desire (and therefore presumably God approves), is more readily achievable by both laity and clergy. The minister can identify himself with the people with less sense of the over-againstness of the gospel by implicitly assuming that his calling is to consent to the consensus that exists, and to be its servant.

There are, however, two possibilities for a critical moral witness that are greater under the conditions of homogeneity. The first lies in a basic simplification of task, due to the relatively uniform culture that is present among the constituency of a congregation. Minister and laity alike can have a more thorough self-understanding of the one culture represented, in part because it is not incumbent upon them to know many cultures represented in the heterogeneous group. In suburbia, for example, there is no reason why a minister cannot study most of the literature on the contemporary American suburb, its social structure, its tastes and values, the occupational orientation that is present among husbands, the particular patterns that marital difficulties take, and the characteristic patterns that idolatry has in this social milieu. The same self-knowledge can be fostered within the church among its members. The understanding, critique, and constructive possibilities of suburban existence in the light of the church's ministry ought to have a sharpness and pertinence that are increased by virtue of the focus on one subculture. The same would be true of rural communities.

The second possibility exists in the middle and upper-middle class congregations. This is an access to influence upon persons in positions of social power. The persons who exercise social power through the decisions and policies of governments, voluntary associations, corporations, and universities or colleges, are often members of Protestant congregations. Acceptance of this social fact as an opportunity does not imply surrender to an individualistic orientation in the church's ministry. A Peale, a Samuel Shoemaker, a Billy Graham, seems to isolate the person from the complexities of his involvement in the world on the assumption that a religiously and mentally healthy man can change the structures, or ignore them. Because they do this does not mean that no other way to deal with middle- and upper-class churches exists. On the contrary, the church can help the person in a position of power to interpret and understand his job, and his exercise of responsibility, as a place for moral action in the society.

The homogeneous congregation need not be accepted simply

as the fate of population movements, nor the manifestation of
the shallowness of American Christianity, though in part it is
both. It can be seen as a gift of mixed value, but nevertheless one
in which the task of the moral witness of the Christian faith needs
to be made under more seductive circumstances, and with some
potential impact upon the wider society.

A sociological framework is only one in which a moral assessment of the voluntary church can be made. Social conditioning is
not a uniformly bad influence on Christian moral community.
But a study of it raises the further problem of authority and consensus, for the churches live under an authority that cannot be
equated with majority rule.

Authority and Consent in the Voluntary Church

Voluntary churches have always had grave difficulties with the
problem of authority in the church, and much more so when the
will to belong replaces the theological principles of the gathered
churches. In the earlier periods, and even today in the lively sects,
there was and is a consent to objective norms of belief, conduct,
and experience. With the absence of clarity about what the contemporary voluntary church is gathered around, or by whom it is
gathered, the danger of anarchy in some important spheres of its
life is ever present.

It is argued by many that the very idea of a "voluntary"
church in a democratic sense is theologically false. P. T. Forsyth,
a defender of chastened congregationalism, suggested that the
church is an absolute monarchy, with Christ as its King, and thus
echoed some of the seventeenth-century fathers of his church. The
church is called into being by Jesus Christ, as each of its members is led to it by the divine initiative. The church is ruled over
by Jesus Christ; it has no other Lord but Christ, and all earthly
church power and authority is derived from him and is under
submission to him. This tends to imply that we belong to the
church by consent to participate in and be ruled by Christ, and
not by our collective judgment achieved through the processes of
democratic voluntary societies.

The rather normal tensions in voluntary associations between
the responsible participation of the members and the initiative

and power of the leaders is quite a more complicated issue in the church. For in the church both the leaders of the congregation and its members consent to a higher authority. This higher authority does not exist by virtue of its authorization by lower authorities, nor is it simply encompassed in some constitutional formula. It is a Person, known through scripture and tradition, but in a living way never completely reduced to them. In this section our concern is with the more visible and tangible aspects of the issue of authority; in the following section we shall be concerned with the more exclusively theological dimensions.

An interpretation of the church as a moral community requires that three points of attention be kept in mind. One is the objectively given sources of insight and norms for the community —the Bible and the writings of the tradition. Another is the vast body of those who are members by virtue of the will to belong. The third is the position of the "expert," or the person whose function it is to define the purposes of the church at various levels of specificity, and to bring persons into consent to them. How are these three actually related in the American voluntary church? What possibilities are there for the development of a moral community in these relations? The American situation might be seen better if contrasted with a vignette of the far less voluntary national churches of Protestant Europe.

Where there is a creedal and liturgical pattern in a national church, to which the overwhelming portion of the population belong by virtue of baptism and confirmation, the clarity of objective norms exceeds most of the documents and patterns of life available to the voluntary American churches. The American exceptions would be Lutheran and Episcopal churches. In the national churches the liturgy contains an explicit theological pattern, including the confession of faith in one of the historic creeds. The clergy receive their appointments with at most the assent of the congregations, and are not dependent upon the continued personal support of the people to stay in office. The relatively high degree of autonomy of the clergy in relation to the people enables the minister to speak from the framework of scripture and creeds without any particular concern for the cultivation of explicit consensus on the part of the members of the church on any particularized issue. Behind this is assumed an objective rightness and truth of the word proclaimed in the church. The net effect is an explicit definition of the purpose and mission of the church in traditional terms, a clergy whose responsibility is defined more in relation to this tradition than it is in relation to the people, and a congregation that is passive in its assent to the authority of creeds, liturgy, and clergy. One effect is the absence of those elements of voluntary life that make the American Protestant laity responsible for the definition of particular purposes and activities in the church. The absence of voluntarism minimizes the activity of the laity. It also makes the life of the church less specific in its relevance to the moral actions of the people, and the life of the clergy simpler (unless they are plagued by problems of conscience and theology, as many are) for they need not develop a lay consensus.

The American voluntary church makes for a more complex working arrangement between the communal norms established by the Christian community in history, the role of the interpreting "expert," and the church members who have the will to belong. *In the complexity given us precisely by the voluntary character of the churches lies the vitality of American Christianity.* First, a description of the processes of authority and consensus in voluntary churches is called for; then the assertion that this is a major asset of the American Christian movement can be defended.

Two important factors make *consent,* rather than assent, the characteristic intellectual and personal relationship between the laity on the one hand, and the interpretation of the normative principles on the other. The first is inherent in Protestantism itself, and more so in the more radical Protestantism of the United States. Protestants claim, and rightly have, a direct access to the norms. They have been given the responsibility as individuals and as persons gathered in congregations to have personal faith, personal knowledge of the God represented in the scripture and the creeds. Casual assent to doctrine, to the objective and external authority of the church, and to the words of theological or ethical experts is foreign to the sense of personal acknowledgment and participation in Christ and his church that is at the heart of Protestantism. Entailed in the expectation of personal faith and responsible participation is the possibility of heterodoxy: of interpretation, understanding, and experience that is somewhat marginal to the traditionally normative proclamations and expectations of the church. For example, out of the serious responsibilities thrust upon the gathered Congregationalists of New England came Unitarianism, partly because of the Protestant expectation of personal experience and reflection upon what is proclaimed by the church and encased in its documents. The expectation of personal response entails the possibility of diversity in the interpretation of the object to which men respond, and requires that the consensus-forming processes go on in order to maintain consistency within the churches. Mere assent to objective truth, dogmatically defined and proclaimed, and inflexibly dramatized in a particular liturgy, would be foreign to the notion of personal response and responsibility that is inherent in Protestantism.

The second factor in the American scene, historically related to the Protestant cultural heritage, is the pervasive democratization of social life in our nation. Responsible participation in the consensus-forming processes is normative in many institutions of American life. Not only in government and voluntary associations, but even in modern business administration, the maximum participation in decision-making is accepted as a basic principle. To be sure, in many organizations assent has displaced consent; the expert professional authorities formulate the policies or the belief-system, and the membership acquiesces, or is simply propagandized into accepting the opinion of others. But the possibility of revolt exists in labor unions, professional associations, and interest groups, as well as at the polls of governmental election. American Christians do not shed this democratic heritage when they stand in the presence of ministers and the Bible, or of church agencies for social action. They expect to register their dissent from the experts, and even from the norms. They expect to have to be brought into a personal conviction of the rightness or truth of the statements being made, the policies being formed, and the actions being counseled.

The religious and cultural conditions of American Protestantism then maximize the participation of the laity in the consensus-forming processes, at least normatively. Particularly where their own interests are most seriously touched by the actions and proclamations of the church, the laity are quick to express dissent, and to claim exemption from obligations to adhere to what is counseled. The leadership of American churches, then, is confronted with a more difficult but equally more significant task than is often required of the leadership of national churches. The norms—Bible, creed, etc.—must be interpreted in a way that is convincing to the laity. No doubts, dissents, or questions can be ruled out simply by recourse to external authority—whether traditional, rational, or personal. The truth and rightness of the norms has to become an inward truth and rightness, in virtually an existential sense, if the norms are to exercise any compelling power in the thinking and actions of laymen. Thus the American churches are organized in ways that normatively (though not always in fact) can create consensus; that is, they are activized in a host of voluntary age, sex, and interest groups.

The interpretation of the norms is one of the media for consensus formation. Even though this is done by experts (whose degree of expertness varies from the careful biblical scholar to the inspired evangelist or prophet for whom everything is prima facie obvious), it is not convincing on the basis of the credentials of the interpreter alone. The points of reference within which the "expert" does his work in part define the acceptability of what he has to say. For example, few laymen would quarrel with a minister's interpretation of St. Paul's view of law relative to the Jewish understanding of Torah, for few would claim the competence to dispute it. But should the minister choose to interpret the law of love in relation to the problems of international relations, or of social welfare legislation, he is inviting dispute with the laity. The political and social points of reference of the latter are in a sphere in which the layman believes himself to have competence at least as great as that of the clergy, and usually more so; they touch areas in which his personal interest and conviction are involved; and they represent a more particularized moral and social judgment than the issue of Paul and the Torah. The authority of the religious expert is not granted by virtue of his knowledge and ordination, and therefore neither quiet assent nor vigorous obedience is forthcoming. The leader becomes a person whose function it is *to give guidance to a consensus-forming process,* in and through which particular judgments (including his own) can be clarified and be brought to bear on the relevant points of action.

The size of the sphere within which the consensus-forming process takes place is dependent generally on the breadth of the minister's own concerns, or those of his denomination. A minister of a sect that confines itself to rightly dividing the word of truth with reference only to the Scofield Bible or to a legalistic version of the Christian life, might well develop a moral and religious community with a considerable in-group identification. But the minister and church that seeks to understand the norms in relation to the rightness of policies concerning man's temporal good in society will have to cope with greater diversity of opinion, and will have greater difficulty in coming to common consent. Congregations expect to be convinced, and expect to share in the process by which convictions are expressed in a corporate way.

The voluntarism (in the sense of requiring a consent of the will and the mind) that characterizes American Christianity is sometimes lamented because it entails all the risks of the voluntary church (in the social sense of the will to belong). Thus suburban culture Christianity, or the idolatries of rural pietism, are all possibilities entailed in this basic principle. But it is this voluntarism (in both senses) that also entails the possibility that American Christianity will continue as a *social movement,* and not merely as an esoteric, grace-dispensing, irrelevant-to-the-modern-world, objectified and ossified institution. The requirements of consensus formation (with varying degrees of diversity within it) provide the conditions under which churches can become moral communities, representing the cares and the possibilities made known in the gospel within the life of the American people. The prophetic and yet responsible participation of the churches in the moral judgments and social policies that are part of life in the world has maximum opportunities within voluntary churches.

The exercise and fructification of these opportunities, of course, is not automatically forthcoming from the existence of these conditions. Consensus is not developed until the norms of the Christian movement are taken with seriousness in relation to life in the world. The training of leadership for voluntary churches requires not only understanding of the group processes, and the effective means of communication, but also of the norms of the church on the one hand, and the issues in the world to be spoken to and acted upon on the other. But there is no stronger reason to despair about the problems of culture Christianity (which exist as strikingly where the norms of Christianity are preserved with a kind of museum-like purity in other parts of the Western world) than there are reasons to view voluntarism as a major asset of American church life. One cannot conjure an easy alternative to the voluntary church that would potentially be as significant in the development of a Christian moral community. Voluntary churches are the agencies in which the more objective norms of the church are interpreted and given consent. In the complexity of the consensus-forming process, given by the voluntary character of the churches, lies the vitality of American Christianity.

God's Presence and Human Consensus

Behind the confidence that American Christianity has in the voluntary churches there lie two possible directions of theological assumption. One is that God is so remote, and so silent, that the life of the church is dependent upon the human cogitation and action that take place in the democratic processes. The formation of a moral community in this case is the effort of a socially contracted group who agree to certain basic principles and seek the implications of these in the areas that require moral decision. This assumption is, probably, regnant within American church life, at least in the churches deeply affected by the Enlightenment and its aftermath.

The second theological assumption is that God is present, and is seeking to speak his word in the life of the church. Although one cannot claim full confidence that the moral consensus of the church is the voice of God, nevertheless his Spirit is present in human deliberation and action. The moral community is called into being by its Lord, nurtured by its participation in his life, and guided by its understanding of his present living Word in and through the life of the congregation. He has witnessed in the prophets and in Jesus Christ, in the events of Israel's history, and in the history of the church. Scripture points toward him, what he seeks to do and what he seeks to say. The moral community is a religious community in the sense of a community gathered in faith, trusting in God and loyal to him. Its deliberation and action are expressions of its efforts to discern God's will and way. The voluntary congregation seeks to walk in the way of the Lord. It has a living Lord who leads it.

All the moral and historical realism of our time tends to make us skeptical of (1) assuming that God can speak through the socially conditioned moral community of a congregation, and (2) assuming that if he did, any difference would be made. We have come to view the church as a human community more under the aspect of sin than of grace; its idolatries are clearer than its obedience to God; its institutionalization is more visible than its moral dedication; its human initiative and activity are more obvious than God's creative and redeeming presence. We are drawn further into doubt by the kind of confidence congregations who really believe that God is present and speaking have in the judgments that they make collectively as groups, and personally as members of groups. In the light of these considerations, we are more likely to defend theologically the *critical, limiting* effects of the consensus-forming process. Just as in Reinhold Niebuhr's famous aphorism about political democracy, so with reference to the church, we are likely to see that the capacities for injustice make voluntaristic churches necessary. Critical voices in the consensus process keep the natural dispositions of the pseudo-Christians from being paraded as divinely authorized. Many theologically alert American Christians do not have confidence in the historical presence and the continuity of God's forgiving and renewing activity made evident in his earthly presence in the humanity of Jesus Christ, and witnessed to by the resurrection narrative. What they perceive is God's absence.

The theological viability of the voluntary church can be substantiated only by a new examination of both the doctrine of the church and the life of the church. Persuasive evidence is more difficult to find pertaining to the latter than the former, but affirmations can be made in both respects.

Doctrinally, the voluntary church is a possibility because of the actuality and the *universality* of the presence and power of God. Traditionally, the defense of the voluntary church has been made more in terms of the *particularity* of the presence and power of God among the gathered saints, who have personally experienced and known his judgment and redeeming grace. A Christian was discerned by certain faithful visible signs to be one whom God elected—religious experience, moral rectitude, and correct belief. These signs were his admission ticket to the fellowship of believers, and his church membership was a declaration of obedience and a submission to discipline. The confidence expressed was finally in the lordship of Christ over all things, but a lordship exclusively mediated to those who testified to its presence in the visible signs. Thus the confidence in voluntariness was limited to the few, and the temptation to assume a moral and spiritual superiority was often too great to resist. The churches felt they could virtually legislate for the society—witness most recently the prohibition of the production and sale of alcoholic beverages. A strong moral consensus could be developed, but it was generally within such a narrow sphere of reference points that in effect the universality of God's ordering work and redeeming grace was denied.

The stress on the particularity of the presence of God to the gathered community of regenerate believers has led more often to exclusiveness and to narrowness in moral outlook than to responsible openness to the world. As the believers in historical apostolic succession assume that there is a particular channel of special grace running through the history of the church, so the exclusive voluntary church tends to assume that the forms and manifestations of God's ordering and redeeming work are confined to those who have voluntarily submitted themselves to Jesus Christ in a particular way. Implicit in this ecclesiology is the assumption that Christ really did not die for all men, but only for those who have had certain experience of his presence. Implicit also is the failure to realize that the risen Christ is Lord over all things, and not just over the things pertaining to individual life and the salvation of individual souls.

The Puritans were an exception to some of these distortions, for the Christ known in the church and acknowledged by the gathered congregation was Lord over all. Their gathered churches sought to define the import of the God known in experience for the life of the world around them. But within the assumption of a differentiating, virtually visible status given to the saints was the temptation to take a magisterial rather than ministerial attitude toward the world. That is, the community of the elect might well claim too much for itself in defining what is the right and the good for the humanity of which it is a part.

In contrast to the assumptions of the gathered church, the doctrinal possibility of the voluntary church lies in the universality of the presence of God, of his ordering and restoring activity in the realm of the temporal, the spatial, the human. Congregations are gathered around the one Lord, expressing through their participation not only the promptings of his Spirit, but also their will to belong to him. Church members are those who will to participate in the life and knowledge revealed in Jesus Christ, and in his people. Neither their presence nor their absence conditions the ultimate reality of God's presence in the church and the world. They are gathered to One who lives and rules in spite of their cultural conditioning, their waywardness, their organizational activities, and their distortions of his will and his way. They are gathered to him through various sorts of religious experience, and in various states of clarity or confusion about the meaning of God's will and way for man. The basic foundation of their being together is not their own social contract to come together, but the objectivity of God's work, the universality of his reign, the particularities of his proffered forgiveness of each man and of men together, and the promise of participation in the newness of life made known in Jesus Christ.

The *voluntary* character of the church, then, does not have its first importance *theologically*. The first order of theological importance is not attached to the human will to belong, or to the willing acceptance of responsibility as a community to God for other men. The first order of theological importance lies in God —the person, the power, the ordering work, the reconciler. The *acknowledgment* of him is the basis of belonging—an acknowledgment that brings with it the personal dimensions of fidelity and confidence in him. The voluntary principle as manifest in the consensus-forming process is of the second order of importance, and can be seen as one of the ways by which those who acknowledge God are brought together in a common understanding of what God wills *of them* in their situation of responsibility. If one can restore the significance of the word practical to the high status it has in the Kantian use of the "practical reason," one can say that the voluntary character of the church is of practical importance. It is the human organization of life through which a Christian moral community can come into existence, and from which influence and action move into the world.

The acceptance of the principle of the voluntary church as a practical principle may help to keep the points of reference open to the world. On the one hand, when the voluntary principle moves toward the first order of theological importance in the definition of the church, the consensus of the community begins to take on a rigid, legalistic, and finally idolatrous character. When *assent* or submission to the consensus becomes the line by which the distinction between the in-group and the out-group is sharply drawn (the saved and the unsaved, the saints and the sinners) , the sphere of its references is reduced, and tendencies toward a false exclusivism occur. On the other hand, when the practical principle of voluntariness is *not* taken seriously, the members of the church either (1) simply participate in the objective dispensing of law and gospel, or the means of grace, or (2) bring no sense of obligation to explore the meaning of the gospel for the common life of man, and thus they simply reflect the consensus of their class, ethnic group, or political and economic ideologies.

The consensus-forming processes take place in the human activities of the churches, and if related to the universality of the lordship of Christ they necessarily include the serious consideration of the spheres of human responsibility outside of the church. They are parts of the media of the mission of God's people, part of the vocation of God's ministry in the world. Their ideological dignity lies in their practical function (for it is not necessary to assume that anything that is practical has no theological dignity!) . Just as so mixed a moral character as King David could through his violent and gracious actions become the practical means by which God's will and way were both made known and actualized in the life of Israel, so also so mixed a moral community as the voluntary churches can become a means of God's will and way in our time. Just as so doubting a person as Jeremiah could be sure both that God put his words in his mouth, and that the day he was born was worthy of a curse, so the mixed human community, seeking to come to a common life in our time, can be responsibly prophetic. As the very manhood of Jesus, with the limitations of culture, of body, and of sphere of relationships and responsibilities, could become the means of God's self-disclosure, so the human practical principles of voluntary church, with their own severe limitations, can embody something of God's presence and God's way.

The concerns of those gathered around the universal reign of God are as extensive as that reign. Yet the actions are set by the conditions under which men live, as precise and limited as the spheres of life extending out from the congregation permit—politics, urban problems, civil rights, consumer mentality, disarmament, alcoholism, and business policies. The pertinence of the moral consensus is related to the concreteness of the human involvement of the congregation. This is a part of the dignity of the practicality and limitations of a human Christian community. The particular social situation of a particular congregation puts the teeth into its moral consensus. Dostoevski indicated that it is easier to profess a universal unbodied love for all men than to love the man in the same room who blows his nose too loudly and sneezes too often. A moral consensus developed with reference to the annoying issues in which self and group interest are involved is prophetic in the great tradition of the prophets.

The practical theological dignity of the voluntary church is no mean one. It provides some of the concrete human materials in which God seeks to speak and make his order known. The voluntary character of the church is important, for apart from the attention that men give to what God is doing and saying, the vineyard God has sowed produces wild grapes. The voluntary American church at its best joins on the one hand the sociologically conditioned character of life with, on the other hand, the divine presence and word of God in a morally significant consensus-forming process.

Foundations
of
Ministry

What constitutes an adequate institutionalization of the intentions and purposes of the Christian faith in our society? This is the basic question to which I would like to attend, although its implications are far more widespread than can be dealt with here.

Institutionalization of Religious Intention

One assumption in this question needs to be made clear. It is that religious faith and religious and moral leadership *must be* institutionalized in any society, and particularly in a highly organized society such as our modern industrialized and urbanized American one. To assume otherwise would be a sociological mistake. That is, any ideas or beliefs, whether they be religious, political, economic, or whatever, become culturally and socially effective through the social organizations and the social forms that they seize upon or grow into. Even if one would choose to crusade against religion being organized into denominations, congregations, and bureaucracies, one would by necessity organize the crusade, secure the necessary funds to keep it going, find the occasions in print or in speech to propagate it, and develop the organization through which it could be continued. To assume that religious and moral leadership do not need to be institutionalized would also be a theological mistake. The realities with which faith deals are always mediated through human and historical forms, through persons, through texts, through communi-

ties, and through events, all of which have "secondary causes" as
well as some basic theological significance and importance. What
is popularly called "spiritual" exists in and through "fleshly"
forms and beings; what is relatively constant in its substance, such
as Christian theological affirmations, is relatively changing in the
words, institutions, and other forms that embody and express it.

This assumption about the necessity of institutionalization
does not imply a defensive interest in the institutional forms that
Christianity has at any particular time, including this time. Indeed, the movement is always seeking, if it remembers that per-
petual reformation is a theological necessity, to find proper re-
institutionalization fitting for certain tasks in certain times and
places.

Institutionalization, however, does not take place in a random
or automatic way. Institutionalization is the effect of decisions
made by religious leaders, by those persons who have influence
and power to give shape to the social structures. Thus my initial
question is a two-sided one: What are the intentions and purposes that can be derived from, or inferred from the root convictions of the Christian faith, from the church's lived experience
of God's grace and God's command? Second, what instruments
are needed for the continuation of the life of the community of
faith, and for the effective realization of its purposes in our time
and our society? There is no simple automatic harmony between
the answers to these two questions. The church cannot decide
what is normative for its purposes and activities simply by finding out what keeps the institution going, what is attractive to
large numbers of people, or what makes for institutional success.
Nor can the church decide upon theological grounds what are
the basic purposes of its ministry, and then suggest that it is a
simple matter to impose these purposes on to the world, assuming
that finances and social organization, for two examples, are pli-
able and formable from the realm of ideas alone.

Our concern is basically to look at some considerations necessary for the adequate institutionalization of *religious leadership,*
and not for other aspects of the process, but the larger issue must
be kept in view.

From the theological side, how do we move from basic affirmations of Christian faith and belief to the formulation of purposes and directives that are to be institutionalized in the churches? When Christian believers affirm something about God and about Jesus Christ, they are not only making statements that "such and such is the case," but also are moving another step, namely, "Because we believe such and such there are certain things we ought to be doing." There are certain "performances" that are demanded by what is affirmed.[1] The procedures for moving from basic Christian convictions to statements of purpose and to deeds then follows a pattern; it has a logic. We can see this logic in three areas of church life.

Areas for Institutionalization

1. Because we believe that the power of life is ultimately good, and it sustains the goodness we know, we ought to praise God, to celebrate the life that he has brought into being, and continues to sustain. Because we understand this power of good in the particular tradition of which we are part, that is, in Jesus Christ and his church, we praise and celebrate God's special gift to man, Jesus Christ; we praise and celebrate the hope we have for the fulfillment of this goodness. All this is to say that the community *intends* to worship. Worship is a performative consequence of the faith and belief of Christians. Then this intention has to be institutionalized in words, actions, forms, buildings, leaders, and music, that are appropriate both to this intention and to the time and place of the church's existence.

2. Because we believe that God wills that men should personally acknowledge him to be the source and giver of life and of forgiveness, we are to invite others to share in the life of the community of faith. We also seek to bring the qualities of human life into accord with this acknowledgment. Thus, in its activity the church intends to be a "deputy" of God, to be an agent of restoration and renewal of life. It preaches and acts in such a way that guilt-ridden men know that there is forgiveness; it proclaims in word and expresses in deed the power of newness of life, and

---

[1] See Donald D. Evans, *The Logic of Self-Involvement* (London: SCM, 1963).

the restoration of life to persons and communities trapped in strife, injustice and hate. These intentions are institutionalized in the preaching, missionary work of the church, in means of communication and expression. These actions are in accord with the trust and belief of the church.

3. Because we affirm that God is good, and wills the well-being of all his children, the church intends to involve itself in the activities and orders of human society in such a way that they become more in accord with the humanity God wills. A moral performance is involved in religious belief. Thus the church intends, through words and deeds deliberated in its own life, and through the activities of its members in the world to help shape an order of life that makes for justice and freedom, for peace and order. This intention is institutionalized in church discussion and action programs, in commissions on racial justice, in statements by church groups on civil affairs, etc.

Other intentions or purposes could be delineated which move in the direction of performing words and deeds that are in accord with basic beliefs. My point, however, is more general. I wish to make clear (1) that faith and doctrine require certain intentions in accord with them; (2) that intentions and purposes take institutional form; and (3) that institutional activities and forms need religious and theological authorization and justification. Without these, not only would the church lose its identity, but other purposes would become the functional substitutes for purposes inferred from Christian belief. Then the church would lose its right object of direction and love, and drift according to whatever interests are most persuasive and best meet particular occasions that are defined according to nontheological standards.

In the process of institutionalization, many other factors come into the picture. To bring them in is not to compromise the purity of intention, but simply to recognize that purposes become effective through *mediation*, through cultural and social forms that can effectively function in the history and culture of the time. Institutions are instruments of purposes. Thus the ministry of reconciliation, of restoration changes its outer garments with the situations of men. When men believed they were plagued by devils that existed as actual spirits, the words of renewal were in the form of exorcism of devils; when men are plagued by guilt that is understood partially in the language of depth psychology, the intention to bring healing takes into account this understanding of man. When Western society was ordered in such a way that the well-being of men could be served by the generous charity of the rich, the intention of the church to meet human needs could be institutionalized in orphanages and Christmas baskets. When both the scope and the complexity of the problems of poverty and their consequences grow, the churches find ways to support legislation and activities that seek to rectify destructive characteristics of aspects of the social order. Whatever the institutional form, however, it must be consonant with, congruent with the purposes and intentions that are the "performatives" of religious faith and belief.

It is at this juncture of theologically directed purposes and their effective institutionalization that the concerns of this paper are located. What are the effective instruments for the church's purposes? We do not begin de novo on this; we have inherited institutions from the past, and we live in a culture that sets the conditions within which purposes can be realized. More particularly, we are concerned with the adequate institutionalization of religious leadership, with personnel problems in the ecclesiastical institutions. The rest of this paper, then, is directed both to interpretation and to some judgments about personnel issues in the life of the church.

Applications to Church Personnel Management

The church, like other institutions with other purposes, has sought to "rationalize" its activity, in the sense that Max Weber used that notion. That is, it has sought to find the most efficient and effective means to achieve its intentions. One aspect of this "rationalization" has been the development of bureaucracies in the church. By and large, Christian groups have not sought to be pure charismatic or spiritual communities, living in the power and freedom of the Spirit alone. They have not relied upon an immediate intuition of what is the right mode of expression of their spiritual life in the particular occasion of human experience. Moves toward the ordering of the social organization of the

church exist already in the New Testament community, and unless one conceives of such rationalization as a mark of the fall of
the church from its pristine purity, in principle one must pay attention to this process and give it guidance.

What has rationalization done in the church? One sees it at
many points, but for our purposes I would like to look at the
increasing division of labor, specialization of functions, which in
turn require specialization of training and competence in personnel. The scope of this division of labor needs only to be suggested: we have theologians and we have educators who try to
make religious life meaningful to preschool children; we have
administrators of funds and of sizable social organizations, and
we have administrators of sacraments. We have experts in race
relations, family life, international affairs, urban problems, evan-
gelism, stewardship and fund-raising, and many more. This specialization runs through all levels of ecclesiastical organization:
the World and National Councils of Churches, synodical or di-
ocesan and conference levels, and into local parish churches.

The Church and Specialization

This situation presents two issues that I would like to state
for discussion: first, a large percentage of the ministers are in
congregations that cannot afford more than one man, or at most
have two-man staffs. Yet the expectations of competence in many
diverse areas of the church's work are present in such a situation.
The minister becomes a general practitioner without specialists
to whom he can refer many of the issues upon which he is expected to make expert judgment, or give significant leadership.
The frustration that echoes from the parish ministers is in part
engendered by this fact. He is expected to give "simultaneous
performance of multiple roles" and purposes, and yet cannot be
expert in any of them. I believe this situation has to be kept in
mind when I turn to two other issues later on, one the insurance
of ample opportunities for continuing education for the parish
ministers; the other is that of the "collegiality of the clergy," that
is, ways of having specialization available with groups of ministers.

Second, the issue raised by the specialization of labor is perhaps more difficult than the first. To put it in the form of a ques-

tion: At what point does the technical instrumental training and function lose touch with the more theologically defined purposive work? This is not a simple question, for obviously its answer would differ with different jobs. For example, if a denomination has a treasurer in charge of not only expenditures, but also investment of funds, his technical competence is clearly the only criterion one might look for, unless one is concerned as some groups are, about the hiring policies of the firms in which investments are made. But to stay close to this example, does one *want a fund-raising specialist* whose procedures are not governed both in the ends sought and the means used by some considerations of a religious and theological nature? Here the issue is muddier, for obviously fund-raising has developed certain technical sides to it, but even some of these may not be congruent with the moral intentions of the church. I believe a memory of the Wells Organization in its heyday ten years ago or more would lift out many details we could discuss in a problem of this sort. Means that were effective became more important than ends. The issue runs through pastoral counseling, social action, religious education, and other areas in addition to the business administration of the church.

Other Issues

There are several subsequent issues, which get closer to actual personnel policy, that the previous discussion in this paper suggests. The issues I have isolated for discussion are in keeping with the concern for personnel policies, and are four: professional mobility, continuing education, collegiality, and financial support.

1. *Professional mobility.* The process of effective institutionalization of purposes requires that machinery be present to facilitate getting the right man in the right job at the right time; or to provide the occasion for the right man to develop the right institutional form effectively to fulfill his ministry. This raises the question of professional mobility. Mobility obviously refers not so much to the "advancement" language according to a scale of social prestige, as it does to location in time and place of the right personal servant to use the proper impersonal structures effectively to fulfill purposes of the church.

The givens we are dealing with here are obvious. There are the diversity of gifts that men have when they embark on their careers in the church, the diversities of talents—some men having fewer and some having more. There are also the diversities and training and experience that religious leaders have. There are also the various openings in congregations or other ecclesiastical organizations, and the possibilities of creating new posts in accord with particular talents that are available.

The institutional problem is how to facilitate the placement process. There is no one single criterion that is available to make the right match, obviously. Ministers, like other men, are capable of self-deception, and often over- or underestimate their ability for particular jobs. Furthermore, they are allured by whatever sirens seem to draw them toward the self-fulfillment of some image of themselves. Thus they want often to be counselors when they need counseling, to be teachers when they have been relatively untaught, or become participants in experimental ministries when they have been unorganized characters in structured ministries.

We have operated in the institutional framework of the ecclesiastical world without the means to make any more adequate estimates of the abilities of men than they have of themselves. Placement dossiers often are filled with remarks that stretch the truth in the name of charity, or are filled with responses necessarily vague and ambiguous because the questions asked are vague and ambiguous. The best things that are done are often done on the basis of the informal systems of social relationships, whereby the people who know the right people and are known by the right people might find the right place. But often the qualitative difference between the visible and the nonvisible person are not that great.

Particularly, there is a moral dimension in professional mobility that I wish to call to attention. Are there any "oughts" left in the church's personnel relations? By this question I wish to suggest that the purposes of the church sometimes require that ·jobs be done that do not enhance personal prestige, a sense of self-realization, or the pleasures of family life. For example, declining rural communities need the church's ministry, but not many well-trained and effective men find Musselshell, Montana, a pleasant place to live. Foreign mission boards, I know, have been plagued by problems that have emerged when the only call was a sense of duty for which there was no coordinate inward ability or motivation. This warns us against denying the importance of personal predeliction and drive. But ministers (like others) and churches often appeal to their own aspirations as the criterion for where a man belongs. There is, however, no automatic harmony between what the purposes of the Christian church demand normatively, and what any one of us would like to do empirically. While there is no necessary virtue to authoritarian constraint, justified by a decision about where the greatest need is, there is also no necessary guarantee that the purposes of the church will be fulfilled when each one of its professional servants is in the place he would *most want* to be.

The complications of professional mobility are increased by the differences in political structure of the denominations, the different relations that exist between freedom and authority. Assignment is accepted by Methodists and Jesuits, rebelled against by Baptists and United Church of Christ personnel. Unfortunately, there is no obvious evidence to prove that the church's purposes are better fulfilled either by a free market personnel economy or by a centrally controlled personnel economy, though this is worthy of study. Presumably in either case it would be possible to bring to bear the theologically directed purposes and the human and institutional factors. It is my guess that greater centralization of authority will be necessary rather than less. Standard Oil of New Jersey *sends* men to Arabia if men are needed there; the church may have to find ways to send men to Musselshell, Montana.

2. *Continuing education.* Much experimentation is being done in this area, and it need not be rehearsed here, nor am I the man to rehearse it. I would raise some questions of what kind of continuing education is appropriate within the framework of the earlier part of this chapter. What continuing education is needed to make personnel more effective instruments of the purposes of the church? Do we collapse continuing education into a kind of therapy for frustrated religious leaders, in which the

basis of analysis of their problems and their functions is determined by the language and concepts of psychology, or sociological
role-analysis? I hope not, for two reasons: (1) ministry is purposive activity, governed within theological affirmations, and this
remains normative; (2) religious leaders are human beings capable of purposive activity, and responsible for what they do and
do not accomplish to some extent. Often, I am persuaded, some
of the means of analysis used in some continuing education enables ministers to locate the problems of their careers as exclusively or at least dominantly "out there," in institutions, or suburbia, before which they seem to be helpless. This can lead to
a morally weak posture of self-pity, of bitterness and hostility,
rather than to some genuine repentance and maximization of the
possible pliability in modes of action.

I am no more concerned with continuing education for the
study of *theology* for its own sake than I am in psychological or
sociological reductionism. What is needed is curriculum, and sufficient theological study to keep the eye on the normative purposes of the church, and sufficient sociological, psychological and
other technical study done to forge the purposes into activities.
Both the improvement of specialization and the improvement of
general practice have to be objectives. I believe this sort of objective exists in many good programs that now exist.

How is continuing education to be institutionalized? That
problem does not need to be solved here: whether in seminaries,
universities, separate institutes, etc. There is, however, an issue
related to the financing of continuing education that ought to be
noted. What has to be done to provide for financial support for
many not-so-affluent ministers and staff people so that they can
attend continuing education programs?

What also is to be done to provide the free blocs of time for
the busy denominational official and the overworked pastor to
gain freedom from his duties to meditate, reflect, and study while
in and on the job? This is an institutional personnel problem of
some magnitude. Its importance can be seen simply: with the
things that need to be done from day to day, one can be occupied
sufficiently, and fail to reflect adequately on the purposes of all
the activity. Helter-skelter activity, directionless in character, is

likely to occur in most professional lives where neither institutions nor personal self-discipline provide time for reflection, study, and reorganization of the self around its normative calling.

3. *Collegiality.* Many ministers are isolated and lonely men, even when not geographically distant from other pastors or administrators. Just as departmental meetings in a university become occasions for significantly political and administrative activity, so many meetings of the clergy become merely occasions to take care of relatively external items of business. Or given the absence of leadership, they become the kind of gripe sessions one hears at cocktail parties and in washrooms. Even staff members in local churches and denominational and other offices, rarely nourish each other's minds and souls. What institutionalization is necessary to provide the sustaining and informing collegiality among religious leaders? Who keeps the lonely general practitioner, or the isolated specialist within a perspective of critical evaluation, or stimulating motivation, or informing insight? What occasions are given that enable the person to reflect with and for and before others about the assignment of priorities in use of time, the clarification of the purposes and means of instrumentation needed for effective church life? Sociological community studies indicate that ministerial associations are laughable in local communities; yet the ecumenical spirit ought to enable both an extension of those involved and a deepening of the issues discussed.

Can we move to enough centralization of authority to see that among the parish clergy in each major center there are varieties of specialization, and thus supplementation for each man's own work? Can we break the denominational barriers so that not every congregation is trying to do every job? For example, is it possible to have *a* good Sunday church school with expert leadership serving several congregations and denominations, rather than having six mediocre or poor ones?

4. *Financial support.* This is not only a matter of comparative salaries with other professions, or of meeting personal and family needs. It is a matter of providing sufficient resources so that the minister does not become intellectually and culturally impoverished for lack of a decent salary. Books, concerts, records,

and travel expenses to good continuing education programs, all are important in providing the occasions for deepening the purposes and making more effective the practices of the church.

Personnel policies for the ministry need to keep in view the intentions of the church as these are directed by its faith and belief. Institutionalization in the church, as elsewhere, is finally merely instrumental; it is to provide the openness whereby innovation is possible, and the channels through which purposes can be made socially and personally and historically effective. Terms used in management studies, such as efficiency, allocation of resources, etc., are not irrelevant to thinking about effective religious leadership. The point of reference, however, that finally governs these things needs to be kept clearly in view: it is not personal self-fulfillment, nor institutional growth; it is the effective institutionalization of what the Christian gospel enables and compels the church to be and do.

Two Requisites for the American Church: Moral Discourse and Institutional Power

More than most theologians of my generation, I quickly become weary of the parlor game of finding out all the things that are wrong with the church in America. I can play the game, and can be as cynical as the next man. But there are many reasons why the game, elevated to a national sport for Sunday supplement readers and for the popular religious book market, tires me. Two of these reasons are most important. Much of the posture of criticism is (a) unconstructive with reference to alternative courses of action for the churches, and (b) unrepentant in its disposition. By the latter I wish to suggest that, like all human beings, the clergy and the theologians are more comfortable if they can blame what is wrong on forces outside themselves. If the problem is a big cultural problem, there is little that Pastor Burton or Theologian Gustafson can do about it; if it is a problem of urbanization or suburbanization or institutional ossification, we little men are at the mercy of apparently hypostatized social processes that inexorably move forward without direction by human agents. Clergy and theologians can find as good excuses as any man to deny any responsibility for what is happening to the community and mission with whose leadership they are charged. If there is a sense of repentance, it is all too often, like a general confession of sin, vague and undifferentiated. It leads to a certainty of guilt for the ills of the church but does not move in the direction of overcoming those ills. Or if it moves forward, it is often less than careful in the clarification of intentions and purposes for the church, and particularly of what the performative imperatives are for the ecclesiastical institution.

As long as there is a religious faith that is shared by a group of people, there will be institutionalization of religion. As long as the religious faith shared by people has continuity with a long tradition, the determination of its future will be in part informed by its history, its past. Since social change is a universal phenomenon, heightened in intensity and extensity in our century, the religious community necessarily seeks new forms and ways to exercise its purposes. Thus religious institutions spawn new forms, find new methods, alter ideological content, revise procedures, in order to survive, and in order to affect positively the social order of which they are part. All of this can go on haphazardly, or it can be given some conscious direction; the church can go on being the passive reactor to whatever ideas, social changes, and moral changes occur, or it can come to some clarity about its purposes and find fitting ways by which purposes can be institutionalized to become effective in the human community.

Thus, I wish to look at the church as a moral community, not in the sense of being actively involved in social change, though I adhere to this too, but in the sense that its own internal life is or ought to be analogous to the life of a serious moral agent. Much could be included in such an interpretation of the church, but I will restrict my considerations to two points. The conscientious moral man achieves some clarification of his intentions, his purposes, his judgments, his ends. He is not just a reactor, but an initiator in the determination of events. The conscientious moral man also acquires the means necessary to actualize his intentions, to achieve his ends, to fulfill his purposes.

If the church is to function effectively, it must come to a clarification of its intentions, its purposes, its ends; it must know how to make responsible decisions about these things with reference not only to its theological convictions and its tradition but also to the particular historical circumstances in which it lives. Thus, it must become a community of moral discourse; moral discourse is a requisite for its existence. The church must also have the institutional authority and the means to achieve these purposes in the society and the historical period in which it lives; institutional power is a requisite for its existence.

Moral Discourse

If one conceives of the church in moral terms, and if one conceives of a moral agent as one who initiates events, who acts on the basis of formulated intentions and purposes, it becomes necessary for the church to learn how to think about its purposes more adequately, carefully, and particularly. At this point, I would include in "church" every level of the existence of the institutional life: local congregations, synods, general assemblies, denominational boards and staffs, and ecumenical agencies.

Intentions and purposes can have various degrees of generality and specificity, and it is appropriate that they have such differences. There are biblical and basic doctrinal mandates for certain intentions. Presumably the people of God are to glorify God; they are to love their neighbors; they are to have a "manner of life that is worthy of the gospel." One could find other equally general intentions that are appropriate to a community that confesses that its knowledge of God and its disposition toward the world are shaped and formed by its allegiance to Jesus Christ as his significance is portrayed in scripture and in the church's tradition. Such general intentions can function as a beam of light, as a basic illumination of the direction and way in which the church ought to go. But with all beams of light there are peripheries that have been only partly illuminated; outside is a darkness.

The reflective process needs to become more specific. Not only does the church need to remember that it is called to glorify God, but it also has to think about how God is to be glorified in the last third of the twentieth century. To use terms now common in some philosophical discourse, one can ask, "What are the performative consequences of believing in God?" One is that it is appropriate to glorify him, out of a sense of gratitude, of rejoicing, for the life and newness of life that he has given. But one can move to a greater degree of specificity in performative consequences. "How is God to be glorified by St. Ansgar's Lutheran Church in Harcourt, Iowa, or by Center Congregational Church in New Haven?" The obvious answer is by worshiping him; and so we might well find the routinized, historically authorized procedures for the worship of God. But we might also find that the glorification of God in these towns in our time requires some careful revision of traditional forms of worship, and that God is glorified not only in our specific attention to him in worship, but also in the deeds of the congregation in the community. Thus we need to ask whether God is glorified by socially exclusive congregations, whether that exclusiveness rests upon prejudice toward others or upon the coziness of ethnic and cultural congeniality of North European national groups. The God to be glorified is the universal father, the giver of life to all, the redeemer of all. If this is the God to be glorified, and not the God of the Lutherans, the Norwegians, or the New England Yankees, there is appropriate intention to perform, viz. an openness and inclusiveness in the congregation of the people of God.

If the God to be glorified is one who wills the well-being of his creation, the restoration of its brokenness, as well as the forgiveness of its sins, then there are intentions that are appropriate to these affirmations. These intentions are specified not only with reference to the great proclamations of the gospel but also with reference to what words and deeds of men glorify God, restore the brokenness of life, and renew humanity, in Harcourt, Iowa, or New Haven, Connecticut, or Dibrugarh, Assam. The specification of intention requires moral discourse. It requires not only theological knowledge and acumen, moral insight and imagination, but also knowledge of the persons, places, opportunities, and obstructions that are the place of the Christian church. Specification of intention is not the task of the pastor or ecclesiastical bureaucrat alone; neither of these is sufficient in wisdom and knowledge, and each is too biased to be reliable as the sole source of determination of particular purposes of the church. Discourse involves mutual probing, each participant with his special skills, his gifts of wisdom, his technical knowledge, his powers of persuasion, enlightening the process toward consensus about what deeds and words are worthy of the gospel, what activities are consonant with the faith, what performances are consistent with and expressive of the beliefs of the church.

The church has to be the place of such discourse. If sin in the Pauline sense is hamartia, missing the mark, rectitude in the life of the church is hitting the mark. All too often the church is a chip of wood floating on the sea, its course, its destination determined by the currents it does not try to direct. Its formation of intentions is too often merely reactive; it becomes other-directed and is not a conscious center giving direction to the events of its world. Too often, it responds to new occasions with the panic of a dying man grasping for whatever will enable him to draw even one more breath. Or it shows the fickleness of an adolescent lover, with fully encompassing passions directed by whatever is attractive and lovely at the moment. Moral discourse, through which the specification of intentions and ends, of words and deeds, can come, enables the church to move with some confidence from the ground affirmations of its faith to be an initiating, directing, active community, with a keen awareness of the marks it ought to hit and of the actions it will take to fulfill its purposes. Moral discourse, governed by the affirmations of the faith, enables the church to keep its identity without isolating itself; it moves from the center of its faith and life, Jesus Christ, outward to its community, its world, its culture.

I am suggesting that each congregation become such a discursive community, and that each synod meeting or board meeting become such a discursive community. What are the affirmations about God and his goodness toward men and the world that draw us together as a people of God? What intentions do that faith and those affirmations seem to entail? What performatives do they seem to require? What is the situation in this community, in this culture, with this family, in this century which these general light-beam intentions are to penetrate? What specific words and deeds give concrete embodiment to the glorification of God, to the reconciliation of man to man, to the restoration of a perverted creation? These are questions in a process of moral discourse in which clergy and laity participate. When we begin to take initiative in reflection, we are likely to take initiative in action. We can become an initiating community rather than a reactive community. Perhaps the church will not be as boring to thinking and acting laymen as it often is now; perhaps it will look less like an archaic museum piece and more like a confident community that knows why it exists.

Institutional Power

There is a significant difference between discourse and reflection that lead to clarity of purpose and intention, and action that alters the course of events. If we are to carry our analogy between the church and a moral agent further, we need to recognize that discourse and judgment-making are only one aspect of action. Discourse requires detachment, disinterestedness, dispassion. Action requires an exercise of the will, a movement of the self which alters the objective situation in which the self lives. Action, in short, is the exertion of power, whether it is the persuasive power of the spoken word, the institutional power of the allocation of funds, the appointive power of putting the right man in the right position at the right time, or some other form.

An illustration from the world of business can help us to see what is involved. The Standard Oil Company is very certain about its basic purpose: to make a profit for its investors and keep the institution thriving for the sake of its employees. There are many performatives that are required to achieve such a basic purpose, and there are many auxiliary intentions that support this basic purpose in only a secondary way. Meetings of the Board of Directors and of comparable groups all up and down the line discursively determine the specific intentions to be realized at the refinery in Bayonne, the tugboat and barge system in the New York harbor, and the production quotas in Venezuela. The point to be noted is that once the intentions are fairly clear, there are various forms of social authority and power in the corporation which enable a relatively efficient realization of these intentions. To be sure, there is no absolute power and authority, and such power as exists meets countervailing powers of competitors, government regulations, and trade unions. But there is sufficient power and authority to make such a corporation an initiator in the complex stream of economic, political, and social life of which it is a part.

Do the churches have such institutional power and authority?

On the whole, the answer is *no*. Should the churches have such power and authority? My answer is that they need more than they have, and that they will need more in the next third of the century than they have needed in the past.

Obviously Standard Oil is not the proper model for comparison with the church, or at least it is not the exclusive institution to be used for comparative purposes. Protestant churches are perhaps more like civil political institutions than they are like business institutions. Sidney Mead pointed out ten years ago that the local pastor, indeed that the church leadership in the voluntary church system, has a distinctively political character. Leaders and institutions of the church are dependent upon broad lay (insert "political") support and consequently have to spend a great deal of time developing such support, maintaining it, and utilizing it, while at the same time hoping that purposes and actions are shaped primarily by the kind of normative discourse I have outlined earlier. I would wish to adhere to the importance of this political conception, not only as a legal necessity in the American scene, but as a theological and moral value. But alteration in traditional practice, in the political and economic structures of the churches, is long overdue. I live in a town in Connecticut that is approaching 20,000 in population and is still governed on a town-meeting basis. The last town meeting held to approve the next step in several million dollars of expenditure for extension of educational facilities was attended by no more than about sixty of us citizens. The problem is complex, but one point I wish to indicate is that in North Haven, Connecticut, indeed in the New Haven urban area, we are operating on eighteenth-century rural and village polities in twentieth-century industrial and urban society. The parallel for the churches is, I hope, clear. We are working with town-meeting polities and laissez-faire economics in a society where other institutions and communities have power somewhat in proportion to their defined purposes.

Let me cite an instance of the problem in church life. If the proper intentions of the church which is faithful to Jesus Christ were to be delineated in the kind of normative discourse I have proposed, one directive would be that wherever there are people, there ought to be an agency of the church's ministry. Declining Harcourt, Iowa or crowded downtown Philadelphia, descendants of northern Europeans or of African slaves, prosperous executives and drunken derelicts; these are indifferent matters in the determination of a basic purpose of the church, namely to bring through word and deed the prophetic and healing ministries of the gospel. There is no warrant that can be authorized by theological and moral normative reasoning for not paying attention to any particular group of persons. Certainly both Standard Oil and the Democratic Party, each for different purposes, are aware of the fact that they ought to be where the people are.

The story of Protestant church life in urban America needs to be remembered only by suggesting some of the most general movements. Lutherans and Congregationalists, Presbyterians and Methodists all followed their congenial social groups out of the cities wherever the prospering people went. This was important: the gospel is for the affluent as well as for the oppressed. Twenty years ago, however, some sensitive members of my generation of theological students caught again the vision that the founders of settlement houses and other forms of city ministry had caught earlier. In the heart of America's cities there were thousands of persons who needed the words and deeds that are commensurate with the faith of the church. Why had they so often been forgotten? In part because the town-meeting polities and laissez-faire economics of the churches followed the profitable church market; partly because the policies of the churches were not determined by theologically and morally normative discourse about the intentions that were proper to the church; partly because pastors found greater happiness for themselves and their families by governing their choices according to social norms; partly because most denominations did not have the appointive power and the budgetary power to allocate personnel and financial resources according to normative conceptions of where the churches *ought* to be working. Policies were not governed by proper theological and ethical reflection; the authority and power of the polities of the churches were not proportionate to the purposes they should have had.

Most churchmen shy away from the notion of "efficiency";

they see it as appropriate to Standard Oil but not to the church. But the church will have to accept the notion as pertaining to its life. Efficiency is not a self-contained word; it is always relative to the purposes to which it is joined. One can use resources efficiently to manufacture automobile tires; one can use resources efficiently to actualize the purposes of the church. The standards by which an act is judged efficient will differ in each case: presumably the lowest possible cost per tire is a good measure in that realm; one would not be prepared to say that cost per convert is an appropriate measure for the church. (I would not be averse to suggesting some consideration of this, however, particularly when I see how much money seems to be going into the "religious ministries" at universities such as my own, where if intentions and ends are clear at all, they are clearly vague.) But it is appropriate to inquire whether the institutional arrangement of the American churches is effective (that is, efficient) with regard to fulfilling presently conceived purposes, whether the churches could possibly fulfill purposes that might arise from a more careful determination of its proper functions, and what institutional changes would be required to make the churches more efficient.

I defend the thesis that even for the purposes in American church life which are now assumed, and not carefully examined and articulated, the institutional arrangement is inefficient indeed. A rehearsal of some of the problems needs only to be suggested.

1. *The waste of manpower and financial resources in many declining rural communities* where duplication of ecclesiastical effort is one of the last vestiges of an evaporating localism and provincialism. I would cite the fact that schools consolidate and that retail businesses either streamline or go out of business, while several Protestant churches compete for the loyalty of a small population. Minor doctrinal and liturgical differences that become the rationalization for such situations can hardly stand the scrutiny of hard judgment in this period of the church's history, and they become a luxury the church can ill afford. Population movements, declining interest in church life, and economic necessity will force a reconsideration of this inefficiency in the next

decades as the reactive, rather than initiating, community struggles for survival.

2. *The duplication of "church extension" programs,* of research for and preparation of church school publications, and of other high-cost efforts on the part of denominations. I was recently told by a young pastor in a growing Colorado community that four of the denominations involved in the much-publicized Consultation on Church Union are all initiating moves to establish new congregations in his community. I am certain that this is not an isolated instance. I know that several denominations within that consultation are involved either in new parish-education curriculum formation or in radical revision of curriculum without much regard for what the other denominations are doing. Yet no one seems to have questioned such localist assumptions as that which says every congregation must have its own church school, with teachers cajoled into helping either out of a sense of duty or out of the unfulfillable promise that this will be one of the great experiences of their lives. At this point, I speak as a member of a Christian Education Committee in a congregation.

3. *The duplication of efforts in theological education.* Fortunately, our awareness of this issue increases. It is clear that the content of most courses in the theological curriculum is common to all Christians, and that very often there is no necessary connection between a man's denominational affiliation and the perspective from which he teaches. I am impressed that even when a confessional tradition comes through strongly in exegesis or in theology, the instructor wants to defend his position purely on its scholarly objectivity and merit. My impression, for example, from a year in a Swedish university, is that while exegeses of the New Testament and of theology had a very Lutheran ring to them, the justification was not in Luther but in a more universal appeal, namely, that these scholars and Luther were both correct on the basis of pure scientific objectivity. In theological education, as in other areas, our institutional arrangements are archaic for present conceptions and would probably be even more archaic and inefficient for purposes that can be better defended than many present ones.

In discussing the church, it is as fruitless to assume that there is a unilinear movement from normative purpose to historical actualization as it is to assume that the development of the American state has been shaped exclusively by the ideology of the founding fathers; the relationship is always more complex and delicate. For the church as for other human communities, historical events evoke reformulations of purpose, and historical actualities set both the limitations and the possibilities for the fulfillment of purpose. We are in a position analogous to those of civil rights and other movements; the intention to achieve an open society has been latent in the national dogma for a long time, but a combination of historical factors has had to evoke the realization of the dogma in institutional and political forms. While we objectively interpret our history in this way, none of us is satisfied with what happened in the past, that is, with the failure of the nation to initiate the process of movement from general purpose and intention to historical realization in an earlier period of history. Some of us are no more satisfied that reformulation of purpose and institutionalization in the church will probably come about out of growing economic necessity, out of a declining interest in the Christian faith (put nastily, a diminishing market for a product deemed obsolete).

I would reiterate a basic proposition. Institutional power must be proportionate to the purposes it is supposed to achieve; or to turn it about, normative purposes that do not have proper institutional power wither away. This proposition is as true for denominations as it is for the ecumenical movement; it is as true for coffeehouse missions as it is for parish congregations.

A great deal of the inefficiency of the churches can be interpreted in the light of this proposition. Our institutional arrangements obstruct, rather than facilitate, the fulfillment of theologically normative purposes. The placement of pastors for most Protestant groups is not determined by a critical assessment of the needs of a particular congregation and community but is a matter of finding which arrangements make two parties—the congregation and the pastor—mutually happy. I take it, however, that happiness is not such a major star in the constellation of values which one can discern from a theologically developed conception of the purpose of the church's ministry; I am not saying that a man may not be more effective if there is a coincidence between his happiness and the work he has to do, but that there may be needs, spiritual and moral, in a community that are evaded rather than confronted by the value of happiness. If there are places that *ought* to be ministered to in some creative or traditional form, the church that is the human agency of the ministry *ought* to have enough power, responsibly arranged in its institutional life, to put the right man in the right place at the right time. If "self-support" or, even more, "high-potentiality" in contributing to the treasury of the denomination is a determinative consideration in beginning new congregations or closing old ones, there is something morally wrong with the institutional arrangement of economic power in the church. If new forms of ministry are directed to a very specific need in a very specific period of cultural history, and confessional purity or loyalty either prohibits the development of such new forms or causes competing forms to come into being, there is inefficiency in the use of institutional and personnel resources.

I suffer no illusions about the practical difficulties in dragging the eighteenth-century town-meeting government and nineteenth-century laissez-faire economics of the churches into the last third of the twentieth century. The church is living, however, in a luxury it cannot afford. The family farm is going, the village or open-country school is going, the small independent mercantile company is going, the inefficient producer of various types of goods is going. This is not merely a result of the egocentric perversity of power-hungry men; it is happening because the purposes of highly productive agriculture, of good primary and secondary education, of lowest possible cost of distribution of food, and lowest possible cost of production of goods require new arrangements of institutional power. I am not suggesting that the churches move in the same direction in order to emulate institutions in our society that currently have prestige greater than our own. This would be false idolatry, an aping of men. Rather, I am suggesting that what other institutions understand, and what we have not understood fully, is that effective fulfillment of purpose requires proper arrangement of institutional power. Others have seen this; we have failed to appreciate it.

No blueprint for what the institution needs to become is forthcoming from this pen. The process of such construction is more complex than one mind can comprehend. The formulation requires its own discourse, and its achievement requires its own political activities. I wish only to hasten thinking that is going on, and to stimulate thinking where it has not yet begun. Thus I close with three questions:

1. Have we thought clearly enough about what the fundamental and the specific intentions of the church in America ought to be, or do we merely persist in traditional purposes or react to whatever external questions and pressures are placed upon us?

2. Do we have institutional arrangements adequate to fulfill such purposes when we once have them formulated, or is our stake in what has worked in the past too great for us to change our present structures? Do we simply let purposes evolve out of pressures, rather than initiate their formation?

3. Do we have the inner freedom to rethink and to restructure? Do we have the courage, required by a new structure, to risk some hostility? Or will we be satisfied for the church to be the last vestige of a dying ethos, arousing only the sentimentality that some of us feel when we revisit the country school we attended or the empty store where we exchanged eggs for shirts and overalls?

A moral community is a purposive and initiating community. It is a historical community in that it reshapes its intentions and its forms to be effective at a new point in cultural history. Either we catch such a vision and follow it, or we become an interesting vestige of an age gone by, like the slight remnant of a tail which reminds each of us that we have also had a biological past. Confidence in God and in the gospel, we have; but we are the secondary agency of part of God's work. Ours is the obligation to make that work effective—which is to say, efficient.